Bob McKibben's *Mark* is a must-use commentary, one of the few actually available that combines a solid basis in history and Christian Tradition while making use of *lectio divina*. This commentary makes use of the latest in Markan scholarship, while remaining faithful to the goal — to engage the reader in a deep study of Scripture.

It also reflects a quality of the presentation and scholarship that is going to prove necessary to the developing Christian mind. I am equally impressed with the questions asked as with the focus, seemingly, on mystical application.

Joel Watts

Author of *Mimetic Criticism and the Gospel of Mark: An Introduction and Commentary*, Editor of *From Fear to Faith: Stories of Hitting Spiritual Walls*

Dr. Bob McKibben is a gifted preacher, teacher, and leader of the church. He employees many of his pastoral skills in offering to us his new book, *The Gospel According to Mark: A Participatory Study Guide.* The insight Dr. McKibben shares on the use of *Lectio Divina* (Holy Reading) along with the commentary for each section, provides an open window into studying and experiencing the rich teaching of Mark's Gospel for the 21st Century. The questions offered at the conclusion of each section invite the reader or study group to live into the full meaning of the text, to truly "**Be** the text" as Bob explains in the introduction. I feel that Life Groups, Sunday School Classes, Church leaders, and anyone seeking to discover a deeper wisdom and understanding from God's Word will feel challenged and blessed by taking to heart this fresh study of the Gospel of Mark. This is good news for the church and for all. Thank you Dr. McKibben!

Dr. Cory Smith, Senior Pastor,
Auburn United Methodist Church

Robert C. McKibbens' book, *The Gospel According to Mark: A Participatory Guide,* provides an effective study guide based on a utilization of the *Lectio Divinia*, holy reading, approach to studying this first Gospel. The book, he indicates, is designed to build the participants' faith in Jesus Christ as the Son of God. In fifteen chapters, McKibben challenges the reader to explore the background of the gospel, meditate on it, question it, pray over it and share one's experience in reading it. He provides challenging questions at the end of each chapter that explore how Jesus may have been "at odds" with the religious traditions of his day, with religious leaders, etc and ask how the reader might also be at odds with some of Jesus' teachings as they apply to our present day. The author has drawn well on other scholarly studies of Mark but uses them in a way that enlightens the lay reader without losing him or her in "heavy" scholarship. The reader is encouraged not only to read Mark's Gospel but react to it as one is guided to see the method Mark used to draw the reader into the message of his gospel. This book can be useful for individual study but best, I believe, when explored in a small group study.

Dr. William P. Tuck
Author of *The Church Under the Cross, Last Words from the Cross,*
and *Journey to the Undiscovered Country*

Dr. Bob McKibben's new contribution to the study of Scripture offers the student an interesting synthesis of the practice of *lectio divina* with practical applications to the text at hand. *The Gospel According to Mark: Jesus – at Odds with the World* poses questions that take the reader on a path which weaves the message of Scripture into the reality of everyday life. The helpful list of study resources provided in the appendices, along with a guide for engaging in such a study, will complement and enhance the student's endeavor to learn more about this intriguing and challenging Gospel.

Dr. Nancy Watson, Director of Ministry
Alabama – West Florida Conference
The United Methodist Church

The task of interpreting the Gospel of Mark in a short book is quite a challenge for any writer, but Robert McKibben has done so in his *The Gospel According to Mark: A Participatory Study Guide.* With rapid pace that resembles the narrative of Mark, McKibben walks the reader through the story offering exegetical insight into the conflict that is a key feature of the Gospel. In doing so, McKibben discusses the historical setting of the narrative while appropriating the key passages for today's believers. The bonus of each lesson is the discussion questions that first ask the reader to reflect on the narrative of Mark for its own sake and then on how the events that are recounted in the story touch on today's believers who are still at odds with the world. This study will be a valuable tool for groups who want to grapple with Mark's story about Jesus, especially for those who are taking their first steps into the Gospel.

C. Drew Smith, Ph.D.
Author of *Reframing a Relevant Faith*

THE GOSPEL ACCORDING TO MARK

JESUS – AT ODDS WITH THE WORLD
A PARTICIPATORY STUDY GUIDE

ROBERT C. MCKIBBEN

Energion Publications
Gonzalez, FL
2016

ISBN10: 1-63199-131-0
ISBN13: 978-1-63199-131-8
Library of Congress Control Number: 2016946401

Energion Publications
P. O. Box 841
Gonzalez, FL 32560

energion.com
pubs@energion.com

TABLE OF CONTENTS

Using this Book

This study guide consists of three sections:
1. Introductory information
2. Study sheets
3. Appendices

It is recommended that you first read the *Appendix A: Participatory Bible Study*, to learn the approach to Bible study used in this series. This guide is built around that approach. You may have other ideas, or even a completely different method, and that is fine, but it will still help if you understand the starting point.

You should also have some kind of guideline for how you will approach your study. That guide is going to suggest a process of study, which I'll repeat briefly here:

1. Preparation, including materials, prayer, and opening your mind
2. Overview
3. Background
4. The inner cycle (or central loop): Meditate, Question, Research, Compare
5. Sharing

This is a study process and says very little as such about what you do in each step in the process. It is built on the principles of *lectio divina*, or "holy reading." Let's summarize those principles first and then look at the steps and see how they will help you apply these same principles.

HOLY READING: A MODEL FOR BIBLE STUDY

Lectio divina, which means holy reading, is an ancient practice of studying scripture. There are many ways to practice *lectio divina*. It has been done in many ways since Origen described it around 220 AD. The great monastic traditions of the church further developed it into distinct phases and practices. The basic principle is that reading and studying the Bible should be remarkably different than reading the morning paper or studying Shakespeare. The Bible is a sacred text; it is a *Living Word*. It should not be studied like it is dead pages from history.

When the two men were walking down the Road to Emmaus, they met the risen Christ, but did not recognize him (Luke 24). As they were walking down the road, Jesus interpreted to them all the scriptures. Only later in the breaking of the bread did they realize that Christ was with them the whole time.

Lectio Divina is a practice that, through the power of the Holy Spirit, invites the risen Christ to interpret scripture to us anew. It is a prayerful reading of scripture that expects God to speak once again through his Holy Word. Prayer should influence the way you study the Bible, and studying the Bible should influence the way you pray. In *lectio divina*, it is impossible to tell when you are studying and when you are praying. There is no difference.

This practice is usually applied on small passages of scripture for an extended period of time. However, in this study *lectio divina* is used as a strategy to study an entire book of the Bible. This is somewhat challenging because the scripture text is so large, but the prayerful approach is still crucial to Christian study of the scripture. In these lessons, the ancient practice of *lectio* is blended with modern study methods that take into account the historical, cultural, and literary contexts.

The historical methods are important to us because they help connect us to people of a different time and place who experienced the same God that we do, learned from the same texts, and were led by the same Spirit. We do not study history because we think history is the meaning; we study history to help us meet those who wrote the texts and those who have studied the passages before us.

The lessons in this guide are designed around the four movements of *lectio divina* established by Guigo II, a 12th century Carthusian monk, in a book called *The Monk's Ladder*. He organized the practice around four rungs that help us draw closer to God through reading the Bible.

Reading (lectio): The first rung of the ladder is reading. Believe it or not this is the step most often skipped or diminished. It is important to do the Bible reading for each lesson in order to get the most out of it. Ideally it should be read several times so that you can become familiar with the language and themes of the text. This book is a guide to help you study the Bible. It is a supplement to the Biblical text; the text itself should have primary focus in your study. The steps of the participatory study method emphasize different ways of reading to help the text become part of you as you study.

Meditating (meditatio): The next thing to do is to prayerfully meditate on the text. Dig deep into it. Study the words. Break it down into pieces. In this study this is where the most of the background information is located. Look up words to find their meaning. Notice if there are any words or actions that the Holy Spirit may be leading you to examine further.

Praying (oratio): Third, we learn to pray the text. Use what you have learned from the scripture to formulate a prayer. It may be helpful to write it down. (There are note pages at the end of each chapter.) At the end of each lesson is a prayerful exercise that expounds on one of the themes from the text. Feel free to add your own prayers. This is where the text really becomes alive to us.

In the method used for this study guide, prayer is not seen as simply one part of the study; prayer permeates your study. You start with prayer and listening so that you will hear what God has to say through the text. Then you end by turning what you have heard from God back into prayer. The prayer never ceases!

Contemplating (contemplatio): The last step is the most difficult and rewarding. You have **read** the text, **studied** the text, **prayed** the text. Now it is time to **be** the text. Let it seep into your being. Be still and listen. Make sure you leave some time after the prayer for silence and reflection.

It is said that Dan Rather once interviewed Mother Theresa about her prayer life. Rather asked her, "What do you say to God when you pray?"

Her answer was simple; "I don't say anything; I just listen."

After that he asked, "Well, what does Jesus say to you?"

And Mother Theresa answered, "Oh, He doesn't say anything, either. He just listens."

Listening is what is important. You may not always feel anything, but God is there. Another facet of contemplation is to learn to *do* the text. We cannot be just hearers of the word, we must also be doers of the word. Let the scripture change the way you live your life.

APPLYING THE PRINCIPLES IN PARTICIPATORY STUDY

Preparation

As you begin the study, preparation will involve getting the materials you want to use, then prayer to begin each session of study. Part of this introductory time will be making decisions about the time and resources you can devote to this study. This is also your time of prayer. Before you begin to read, you need to pray. Then you need to listen. You come to the text because God calls you to it.

Overview

Getting the overview is accomplished by reading the Gospel According to Mark through at least once, but preferably three times, and in exceptional cases up to 12 times. Don't feel bad about how many times you read. Choose a number that seems reasonable to you. If you start reading the third time, and it feels like a burden, move on. This is part of *lectio* but only part. You will learn to read in other ways in different phases of your study. Once you have read the Gospel According to Mark through your chosen number of times, read one or two of the following

1. The entry on Mark in a Bible handbook

2. The entry on Mark in a Bible dictionary

3. The introductory note on Mark in your study Bible, if you're using one.

4. The introductory section of a good commentary on Mark (see Appendix B for resource details)

Here is where we introduce historical elements into your study. Don't imagine that God cannot talk to you through this text because you are so far separated from the people who wrote it. They were people like you who had hopes, dreams, gifts, and failings. Study the background to help you connect to them. Christianity is a community that extends not only in space right now but in time.

The Central Loop

For this overview, your central loop, as I call it, is your whole study of the book. Keep in mind that no element of your study is something you do just once and then forget about it. Prayer is continuous. There are multiple ways of reading, questioning, studying, and sharing.

This is most closely related to *meditatio*, but the implementation of *meditatio* extends into the next section where you question the text in a directed way. Don't concentrate on the boundaries between one activity and the next. They are all related!

With each unit there will be an opportunity to try to think of new questions one might ask for further study. Generating new questions helps keep us from getting stale. Not only do I not have all the answers; I don't even have all the questions! Think of a question primarily as a way to prepare your mind to hear the text.

When we listen or read, we often hear what we expect to hear. If I'm listening to the radio for weather, I may miss a major discussion of politics. You can miss what God is saying to you through a Bible writer because you are looking for something else. Questioning is thus an important part of *meditatio*, but it also relates closely to *oratio*—take your questions to God in prayer.

Finally, find something to share. Remember that sharing can be in the form of a question. For example, one might ask others how they understand a particular word, such as "incarnation," "poverty," or "atonement." Take notes on their answers, and bring that information back to your study. Then ask yourself what your neighbors will hear when you make particular statements, such as "I must be bold for Jesus!" or "Jesus is the only way to receive atonement." Do those statements mean something to them? Do they mean the same thing to them as they do to you?

This is part of *contemplatio*, as you try to be and do the text. We often think of sharing primarily as telling someone things that we have learned. But if what you learned is that God loves prisoners, for example, you might find that the best way of sharing that lesson is to become active in prison ministry. Sharing demonstrates that you don't believe the text is your private possession. It is God's gift to the Christian community.

RESOURCES

The following resources are referenced regularly in the text. In a small group it is a good idea to have different members of the group bring different references. For individual study, use a selection:

1. Study Bibles, with particular reference to *The New Oxford Annotated Bible, New Interpreter's Study Bible, The Harper-Collins Study Bible, The Access Bible,* and *The Today's New International Version (TNIV) Study Bible.* These are not the only Bibles that one might want to consult, and while most of these relate to the NRSV, they do represent a range of versions and viewpoints. You can look

for similar articles in your study Bible. I don't use resources from any one perspective. Look at materials you are likely to disagree with in order to stimulate your thinking. (See Appendix B for information on these resources. The Participatory Bible Study web site, http://www.deepbiblestudy.com, is regularly updated with ideas about materials.

2. Concordances, either English only, or those that include material on the original languages. If you get a concordance, find one that is based on the Bible version you use.

3. Bible Dictionaries, which overlap Study Bibles and Bible Handbooks in terms of their use, but which are very useful for general study of topics you may find.

4. Bible Handbooks, used in much the same way as study Bibles, but without the text of the Bible itself included.

5. Bible Commentaries offer more detailed exegetical explanations and interpretation of the actual text than can be found in the other resources. For the New Testament, I would recommend purchase of *The People's New Testament Commentary* written by Fred Craddock and Eugene Boring.

When it comes to comparing passages you will find your study Bible, concordance, and any Bible with reference notes to be very useful. Remember, however, that even the cross-references are just someone's opinion of how one passage is related to another. You don't have to agree. Look at the passages yourself, and ask not just whether they are related, but *how* they are related.

Remember to keep an open mind and a receptive heart while studying the Bible. Study prayerfully. Meditate on what you read. Try to place yourself in the audience of people who might have first heard this book read to them aloud in a small house church.

THE HISTORICAL GOSPEL ACCORDING TO MARK

Since the middle of the second century onward Mark's gospel account was considered an inadequate stand-in in comparison with the other Gospel writers. The early church fathers discounted Mark's importance and placed it second in the Canon and sometimes even fourth. Matthew's gospel was always given preference in the early church, then Luke and John. The Gospel According to Mark was scarcely even an after thought.

Even into the latter half of the 1900s scholars judged Mark to be of low value. Gunther Dehn wrote that Mark was "neither a historian nor an author. He assembled his material in the simplest manner thinkable."[1] Rudolf Karl Bultmann penned these words. "Mark is not sufficiently master of his material to be able to venture on a systematic construction himself."[2] Etienne Trocme ridiculed Mark's gospel, "The point is settled: the author of Mark was a clumsy writer unworthy of mention in any history of literature."[3] These texts were still in use in our seminaries in the 1980's.

Even as these scholars where being recommended to our pastors, the value and place of Mark in modern theology was receiving an extreme makeover. After careful internal investigation Mark was not a plagiarist of Matthew's work, but

1   G. Dehn, *Der Gottessohn. Eine Einfuhrung in das Evangelium des Markus* (Hamburg:Im Furche-Verlag, 1953), page 18.
2   R. Bultmann, *The History of the Synoptic Tradition*, trans. J. Marsh (New York: Harper & Row, 1963), page 350.
3   E. Trocmé, *The Formation of the Gospel According to Mark*, trans. P. Gaughan (London:SPCK, 1975), page 72.

rather authored the earliest of the gospels. While there were no copyright laws as such in the first century, it appears that Matthew and Luke borrowed repeatedly from Mark's gospel account.

Mark's new found rank among the gospels is not unchallenged. But the bulk of recent scholarship has led to a revision of Mark as a clumsy and unworthy writer. As we will see in this study, Mark's gospel account employs some unique literary devices and gives birth to an entirely new genre of literature. Marks gospel outlines a clear theological representation of Jesus as the Son of God.

DATE AND PLACE OF AUTHORSHIP

Because this gospel account comes to us anonymously and undated, the question of authorship is little more than speculation. There is an old tradition that credits John Mark of Acts 12:12 (and 15:37) as the author. According to the legend John Mark wrote the gospel in Rome as a synopsis of Peter's preaching (I Peter 5:13). The rapid fire sequencing of events and the use of everyday spoken Greek gives support that this is a written version of the earliest oral accounts of Jesus' life and ministry.

As mentioned earlier, The Gospel of Mark is now thought to be the earliest of the canonized gospel accounts but an exact date is impossible to document. There are internal references to the destruction of Jerusalem in chapter 13 which could place the writing somewhere between 65CE and 70CE. Many scholars now believe that Matthew and Luke used Mark's gospel account as a primary reference.

In the earliest manuscripts, Mark appears to end abruptly at 16:8. We will look at the ending in more dept later, however some later (but still significantly early) manuscripts add resurrection appearances and other elements to "complete" the gospel.

STUDYING THE GOSPEL OF MARK

Much has been written on *how* to study the Bible. Several books are excellent and give us more than adequate guidance. I suggest that anyone reading this study use the method that best fills his or her personal needs. I will offer these insights, however:

1. *The Bible is the primary text.* As the Word of God the Bible is the principal and fundamental authority when it comes to studying the life and ministry of Jesus. Please be aware that various translations of the Bible come with predetermined "human" theologies, but most are faithful to the primary intent of the author's writings.

I recommend that participants in this study first read the entire Gospel of Mark in one setting, two at the most, prior to launching out further. Look for themes and concepts that jump out for you. While I have given some hints below, write down your own list as you read the gospel. Once into the study, read the passage about to be discussed in its entirety. Please remember that chapter and verse marking along with section titles were not part of the original manuscripts.

2. *This Study is only a Guide.* There are no scholarly claims or authoritative doctrines offered by the author. I intend only to be a facilitator in the study of Mark's gospel account, a pastoral moderator at best. Occasionally, other scholar's thoughts are offered, giving authoritative weight on the matter being discussed, but never intended to establish a point of view that the participant is

required to accept. This study is designed to build the participant's faith in Jesus as the Son of God and offer support for leading a life in Christ. But beware! You may discover that you are at odds with what you learn from the Bible.

POSSIBLE THEMES TO LOOK FOR

JESUS IN MARK
    Found in Old Testament
    Authority
    Servant of God
    Son of God (Son of Man)
MINISTRY AND LIFE OF JESUS
    Conflict
    Spiritual Battle
    Faith and Faithfulness
    Discipleship
    Insiders vs. Outsiders
    Command to Silence/Secret Messiah

PRAYER FOR ILLUMINATION

As part of the liturgy for Worship Services and the administration of Holy Communion, early Christians would often pray for understanding of the scriptures. One such prayer has found its way into present day worship. Even though present day worship has become less liturgical (there are signs of resurgence) the following prayer is still used:

Lord, open our hearts and minds by the power of Your Holy Spirit, that, as the Scriptures are read and Your Word proclaimed, we may hear with joy what You say to us today. Amen.

Study Outline

1. The Coming of the Good News (1:1-13)
2. The Beginning of Jesus' Ministry (1:14-45)
3. Ministry Amidst Conflict (2:1 – 3:12)
4. Ministry to Insiders verse Outsiders (3:13 – 4:34)
5. Jesus Not Yet Revealed (4:35 – 6:6)
6. Ministry to the Jews (6:6 – 7:23)
7. Ministry to the Gentiles (7:24 – 8:9)
8. Jesus Revealed (8:10 – 9:29)
9. Jesus Style Discipleship (9:30 – 50)
10. Judea to Jerusalem (10:1-52)
11. The Conflict Intensifies (11:1-26)
12. Conflict with Sanhedrin (11:27 – 12:44)
13. Tribulation and Triumph (13:1-37)
14. The Betrayal (14:1-72)
15. The Final Conflict (15:1 – 16:8) and Second Ending of Mark (16:9-20)

LESSON 1:

THE COMING OF THE GOOD NEWS

CHAPTER 1, VERSES 1-13

Prayer: *Heavenly Father... Thank You for sending us Your Son, Jesus Christ. Be with us now, as we open our hearts and minds to Your divine scripture. May we find in Your words the truth about Your Son whom we call Lord and Savior. May we also find the guidance we need to walk in a manner worthy of Your calling as Christians. All glory and honor is Yours, Father. Receive this prayer in Jesus name. AMEN.*

In the beginning is how Mark chooses to open his gospel account. It reminds of us of the opening words of the Old Testament found in Genesis. It also is like the opening words of The Gospel of John. While it would be unfathomable to think that Mark used those words knowing he would be opening a whole new testament of God's Word, that is precisely what happened.

While Matthew's gospel appears first in the canonized Bible, Mark is believed to be the first written and circulated among the early Christians. Unlike Genesis, which cites the *beginning* of creation, and John, which cites the *beginning* or preexistence of the Word (Christ), Mark announces the *beginning* of the Good News.

Significantly, Mark announces the *beginning* of the Good News (gospel) of ***Jesus Christ, the Son of God.*** This proclamation stands against any other declaration of good news. For example Caesar claimed himself to be a "savior" who brought prosperity and peace to the world.

Good news, transliterated later into the word "gospel", comes from the Greek word *euangelion, which* is the background for our church application of evangelism and evangelist. Mark thus becomes our first evangelist, proclaiming the "gospel" of Jesus Christ. More significantly, Mark launches a new literary genre in applying the term *euangelion* to the ministry and life of Jesus Christ. Mark's second-class status as a Biblical author suddenly must be reviewed! Mark created the stylistic literature call "gospels."

In the Old Testament and in Greek literature derivatives of *euangelion* were used often to report victories from the front line of battle. (1 Samuel 31:9, 2 Samuel 1:20, 18:19-20, I Chronicles 10:9). Here we find the first hint behind the purpose of Mark's gospel account. A common theme of conflict and battle fills the pages of this gospel. Mark is bringing "good news" from the battlefront to the early Christians. He is giving them encouragement for their own battles of persecution and suffering. Ultimately, because Jesus was victorious, they too will be victorious.

Verses 2-8 introduce John the Baptist. Interestingly, Mark does not offer any genealogy or birth narrative as do Matthew and Luke, but all the gospels include the presence of John the Baptist or baptizer. His introduction provides the open door back into the Old Testament and gives visuals of Old Testament heroes. The verses echo Isaiah who establishes for Israel a messianic future of restoration, peace, and prosperity. John's dress and message reflects an image of the great prophet Elijah who was said to return some day as a forerunner of the messianic age Israel so longed for. The fact that Israel was presently under oppressive Roman occupation made these images of liberation so much more real and Mark's "good news" so powerful.

The scripture text tells us that people from the whole Judean Countryside and the people of Jerusalem were coming to John the Baptist. This has the feel of ministry only to Jews, but this cannot be exclusively the case. Also note that John was **proclaiming a baptism of repentance for the forgiveness of sins.** This sounds perfectly acceptable to our modern ears, but this was not the typical

Jewish message. Baptism for the Jewish people was done on many different occasions for ritual cleansing. Forgiveness of sins was a once a year ritual that took place on the Day of Atonement. John's proclamation would have been considered a bit radical in his day, but yet the people came in large numbers. The combination of John's message of repentance for forgiveness of sins and his popularity ultimately lead to his death.

Verses 9-11 announce the public appearance of Jesus of Nazareth of Galilee. This is the only reference Mark makes of Nazareth with the possible exception of 6:1 where the term "hometown" is used. Mark's account of Jesus is very brief and to the point. The story is offered to make three distinct points: [1] the heavens torn apart, [2] the Holy Spirit descending on Him, and [3] the declaration from heaven (God).

This climatic event becomes the definitive breaking news announcement that the Kingdom of God has come. The baptism of Jesus inaugurates the long awaited return of God's Holy Spirit. It comes with God's personal declaration that "this is my son", the beloved of God. The baptism of Jesus is embedded with all the required characteristic of the long awaited Messiah – the Father's love, filial obedience, Kingship, suffering servant – this is The Son of God! Jesus is the embodiment of the Good News. He is the gospel – the *euangelion.*

Verses 12-13 mark the beginning of the "conflict." The Holy Spirit drives Jesus into the wilderness where God's Son encounters God's adversary. Mark names the adversary specifically as Satan. Mark does not go into detail but simply states that Jesus spent forty days being tempted by Satan. The number forty is used throughout scripture to denote trial and victory, and often renewal. The wilderness is the proving ground of the faithful and those who persevere receive the promised deliverance.

»   Israel spent 40 years in the wilderness
»   Moses spent 40 days on Mt. Sinai
»   Elijah spent 40 days on Mt Horeb

Jesus At Odds:

1. Why does the message of John the Baptist and Jesus qualify as "Good News?"

2. Why was Jesus baptized by John in the River Jordan?

3. What is the significance of Jesus being sent into the wilderness?

You At Odds:

1. How would John the Baptist be received in your hometown – church – home?

2. What do you remember about your baptism?

3. Has there been a "wilderness" event in your life?

NOTES

LESSON 2:

The Beginning of Jesus' Ministry

READ: Chapter 1, verses 14-45

Prayer: *Oh Holy God...Help us to experience Your call upon our lives. Our desire is to praise You and to be genuine followers of Your Son. As we follow Jesus in the opening of His ministry show us how to be true disciples. Here our prayer in Jesus' name. AMEN.*

John the Baptizer is Arrested. Without fanfare Mark reports the arrest of John. He tells the rest of the horrible story later in Chapter 6, but for now it is simply the benchmark that indicates that Jesus is back to begin His earthly ministry. Jesus, like John, called people to repentance, but there is a distinct difference. John called people to a baptism of repentance for the forgiveness of sin so that they could be prepared for the coming Kingdom. Jesus came to Galilee proclaiming the Good News that the Kingdom is at hand. Jesus simply called the people to **repent and believe in the Good News.**

Verse 15 becomes for Mark a summary or thesis statement for Jesus' life and ministry, which is the foundation of the remaining chapters. For Mark, this was the materialization of the long awaited Kingdom of God and renewal of Israel. As the remaining chapters unfold, the extreme price for that renewal and transformation becomes painfully clear.

Verses 16-20 identify the location for the start of Jesus' ministry as shoreline of the Sea of Galilee. While it cannot be concretely established, it seems that Jesus was baptized by John in the River Jordan in Judea somewhere near Jerusalem. Once Jesus completes the forty days of trial in the wilderness He reappears in the Northern Kingdom near Capernaum, which is on the northwestern part of the Sea of Galilee.

Call of the Disciples. Remaining consistent, Mark offers little detail in outlining the call of the Disciples. With little or no adornment he takes just five verses to name four fishermen. What is notable is that all four *immediately* left their nets and followed Jesus. It takes the whole of the New Testament to develop a characterization of the disciples Jesus calls. Mark does, however, drop a little hint as to the personalities of the four. Simon (later Peter) and Andrew were actually fishing while James and John were sitting in the boat mending.

Verses 21-22 opens with Jesus observing the Sabbath by attending the synagogue. The English in the NRSV may be misleading in that it says *he entered the synagogue and taught.* The synagogue was the assembly of the village and not necessarily a physical building much in the same manner that the "church" is not a building but the people who make up that particular gathering. The synagogue would normally have an overseer who apparently extended Jesus the invitation to teach. The assembly immediately realized that Jesus taught with authority (power) that was unlike what they were use to hearing from the Scribes.

Verse 23-26. The content of Jesus' message and the authority with which He taught immediately sparked a disturbance. Amidst the assembly was a man possessed by an "*unclean*" spirit. The term unclean may be a hint that this was an assembly held outdoors. Once the synagogues began erecting meeting structures, those declared unclean would not have been permitted to enter.

While the local people were amazed and astounded by the authority with which Jesus taught they didn't really recognized who He truly was. Shockingly the unclean spirit did recognize Jesus! The demon clearly understood that Jesus had the power to destroy him and also recognized that power as being from the *Holy One of God.*

Jesus ordered the demon to "*be silent, and come out of him!*" The command to be silent is understood by many to be the beginning of a pattern by Jesus to conceal His messianic identity. Mark fosters this messianic secret throughout his gospel account.

» Commands to silence addressed to the demons that acknowledge his power: 1:34, 3:12.

» Instructions not to make his healing-miracles public: 1:43-45; 5:43; 7:36; 8:26.

» Teaching to the disciples in private: 4:34; 7:17-23; 9:28; 8:31; 9:31; 10:32-34; 13:3.

» Commands to silence addressed to the disciples: 8:30 and 9:9.

» The parable-theory, 4:10-13, by which the parables are intended to obscure the message so that outsiders may not understand.

William Wrede contends that Mark uses this messianic secret not so much for shielding Jesus' identity but to establish the reason for the fact that Jesus was not readily accepted as the messiah. Jesus made no public claim to be the long awaited messiah.[4]

The exorcism or the casting out of the demon at Jesus' command was met with an outwardly visible and audible struggle. While this skirmish between Jesus and the unclean spirit surely frightened many, it was also met with astonishment and awe. Mark cites this event as the rapid growth of Jesus' popularity and fame throughout the northern Kingdom. This popularity, as we will see later in the gospel, was the beginning of the religious elite's displeasure with Jesus.

Verses 28-34 provide somewhat of a summary of Jesus' activities in Capernaum beginning with healing of the disciple's family members. Notably at sunset, once the Sabbath was over, many throughout the city brought their sick to the house. Jesus cured many of unspecified illnesses and cast out many demons without much recorded fanfare. Mark makes a point to say that Jesus would

---

4   William Wrede, *Das Messiasgeheimnis in den Evangelie*n (1902, first translated 1971), Ulan Press 2012.

not let the unclean spirit speak, seemingly at risk of revealing Jesus' real identity.

Verses 35-45. At the onset of Jesus' ministry, Mark wants the reader to know that Jesus prayed. The unspoken hint here is that Jesus' power is directly linked to His close bond with His Heavenly Father. Mark also restates his gospel thesis by having Jesus personally declare His purpose to proclaim the message *of the Kingdom of God* [italic mine].

As with the dramatic scene of casting out the unclean spirit, Jesus is now confronted with another "unclean" person, a man with leprosy. The text indicates a bold move by the leper. By Jewish law the leper was to avoid everyone and declaring loudly that they were unclean thus preventing even an accidental encounter. But this leper came to Jesus and knelt before Him, begging Jesus to heal him.

The next phrase has a varied history of translation. The NRSV say that Jesus was "Moved with pity." Some ancient manuscripts say "Moved with anger." Either way, in defiance of the rules established by the religious hierarchy Jesus touches the man and instantly he is made clean. Jesus instructs the man to leave telling no one. Surprisingly, Jesus then instructs the man to go to the religious leaders showing himself clean and to make the offering declared by Moses. Commentators have attributed several different motives for Jesus making this a requirement. Some believe this was a tongue in cheek statement while others believe Jesus wanted to make a demonstrative statement. Still others see Jesus trying to restore the man back into the community. Regardless of the motive, the now clean man ignored Jesus' warning and told everyone, so much so that Jesus and the disciples had to leave.

Jesus At Odds:

1. Give a pictorial description of the Disciples and how do they compare with the people of Jesus' day?

2. What significance do you give to the fact that the first miracle or act of power Jesus performs in Mark's gospel is the casting out of a demon?

3. Why did Jesus instruct the man healed of leprosy to tell no one about it?

You At Odds:

1. Have you ever felt the call of Jesus? How did you respond?

2. Do you believe there are persons in your church who have an evil spirit or demon?

3. If Jesus healed you, would you tell anyone?

NOTES

LESSON 3:

MINISTRY AMIDST CONFLICT

READ: CHAPTER 2:1 THRU 3:12

Prayer: *Almighty God, our Heavenly Father…We want to live strong and fruitful lives for You. We want to be a part of Your Kingdom. Through Your divine Word demonstrate for us what we are to do and how we are to live as followers of Your Son Jesus Christ. In His powerful name we pray. AMEN.*

Jesus' Ministry Brings Controversy. This sounds like a terrible thing to say, but Jesus healing a man from paralysis brings both delight and dispute. This story begins a series of disputes with the scribes and Pharisees. The scribes were what might be called legal experts and provided the Pharisees, a particular class of religious leaders, with scholarly and legalistic support with which to rule over the Jewish people.

Verses 1-12. Once Jesus returned to Capernaum (interestingly recorded as Jesus' home) people once again began to crowd around to hear His authoritative teachings. Among the group were some scribes. During a teaching session a group of men attempted to bring a paralyzed man to Jesus for healing. The crowd was too large, and reading into the story, the crowd was not willing to yield to let the man be brought before Jesus. The four men lifted the paralyzed man onto the roof.

In Jesus' day roofs were often made of a mud plaster formed over a wooden or thatched framework. The roofs would also often be accessible by exterior steps. We know from scripture that the roof was used for sleeping quarters during part of the year. It would have required a certain degree of effort on the four men's part to get the paralyzed man to the roof and to break a hole into the roof, but it wouldn't have required an excessive amount of exertion as it would today. Still, it would have been an extraordinary and unprecedented move on their part.

When the man was lowered through the roof and placed before Jesus, He realized that these men's efforts and persistence were an open display of faith and Jesus rewarded them. Jesus healing the paralytic was in response to all five men's belief that Jesus could and would do so. Jesus not only healed the man, but also took the opportunity to teach an important lesson.

The people of that day, reinforced by the scribes and Pharisees teaching, believed that a person was sick, or deformed, or blind, because of sin in their lives, either theirs or their parents. Leaning on the people's understanding (and probably the man's), Jesus healed him simply by forgiving the man of his sins.

The scribes discussing among themselves immediately accused Jesus of blasphemy! No one but God can forgive sins. Mark provides for us a clear picture of Jesus' spiritual gifts. Jesus clearly discerns the hearts and minds of the scribes and confronts them. Jesus also indicates that He is the "Son of Man." This title carries the meaning of "human, " but also the "exalted one" who will restore Israel. Jesus is both, but here, is claiming His authority that comes from God the Father.

Verses 2:13-3:12 Having confronted the religious leaders on the matter of healing and debating with them concerning blasphemy Mark then takes us through a series of confrontations between Jesus and the Scribes and Pharisees.

Eating with Tax Collectors and Sinners: Levi, who is identified as Matthew (Matthew 9:9), was a "toll collector" in Capernaum working for Herod. That alone made him unpopular, but coming into regular contact with non-Jews and other outcasts made him "unclean" in the eyes of the religious leaders. The religious leaders shunned all who were unclean and those who didn't adhere to their rules (sinners). By association the scribes and Pharisees feared they would be considered unclean and sinful. Not associating with such was part of their brand of righteousness.

Fasting: It is not made clear what the occasion of the fast was, but the religious leaders objected to Jesus and His disciples not observing it. Essentially, they were disobeying the rules set out by the leaders. Sensing this tension, Jesus cited the wedding custom of feasting and celebrating with the bridegroom as an exemption from the fast. The wedding was a traditional symbol of future blessings and fulfillment. For Mark, Jesus is understood as the bridegroom, bringing in something new that was overriding old forms of righteousness. At the crucifixion the bridegroom would be taken away.

Hunger and Healing verse the Sabbath: Once again the Pharisees meet head-on with Jesus and His disciples for violating their rules. It is not made clear whether they were violating the rules on travel or of harvesting. The religious leaders had stipulated an interpretation of the fourth commandment (Exodus 20:8-10) right down to the number of steps you were allowed to take before it constituted "labor." Jesus cited a historical moment when King David violated the rules in order to feed his soldiers. But what followed was one of Jesus' most significant teachings. *The Sabbath was made for humankind, and not humankind for the Sabbath.*

Mark follows this up with a story of healing. Again, it is not clear if this is to be understood as the same Sabbath or another, as Mark is not overly concerned with chronological order. But what we do see if a significant change in the Pharisees behavior. They did not challenge Jesus but rather just watched looking for yet another incident to accuse Him with. Jesus once again discerned their hearts and calls them closer. Jesus was angry, even grieved, by their hardness of heart. Just as when He performed an exorcism on the Sabbath, Jesus did not hesitate. He healed the man's emaciated hand. It was at this point that the Pharisees began to plot against Jesus. The verses that follow are a summary statement of Jesus' ministry of healing and exorcism accompanied with the order to keep His identity quiet.

Jesus At Odds:

1. Why were the religious leaders mad at Jesus for healing the paralytic?

2. Do you think it was right for Jesus to associate with a tax collector?

3. Why was Jesus disrespecting the Sabbath – or was He?

You At Odds:

1. What would have happened in your church if someone interrupted a worship service by bringing a crippled person to the front to be healed?

2. What rules of your church have you broken? Why?

3. What does breaking the Sabbath mean today?

NOTES

LESSON 4:

MINISTRY TO INSIDERS VERSE OUTSIDERS

READ: CHAPTER 3:13 THRU 4:34

Prayer: *Heavenly Father ... You alone are God. You loved us so much that You gave us Your Son Jesus – our Lord, our Savior, and our Friend. And through faith in Your Son we also have received the Gift of Your Holy Spirit. We truly desire to be led by Your Holy Spirit. As we follow the Holy Spirit, lead us away from all that is evil. Protect us from those who would do evil things and may we always acknowledge Your Spirit in our hearts and lives. In the name of Jesus the Christ. AMEN*

Verses 13-19 This lesson begins with Jesus appointing twelve everyday ordinary men to be His disciples. Mark lists all twelve disciples here. The text then reads, "*Then He went home.*" Mark does not make it clear if home this time means Capernaum or Nazareth, but we do have the introduction of Jesus' family. Here in Mark's Gospel account we see that Jesus' family was made up of His mother and brothers. Interestingly, Mark states that Jesus also had sisters, but no names are ever given in the New Testament. The crowd, symbolic of Jesus' growing popularity, once again pressed in on Him.

Verses 20-22 Jesus' family tried to hold Him back from going to the crowd. Their reason is most revealing. Pharisees from Jerusalem (indicating higher up the leadership chain) had come and started their campaign to discredit and demonize Jesus. ***He has gone out of His mind...He has Beelzebul.***

Beelzebul can be interpreted as "Lord of the house" (i.e. house of demons). A possible hint is that Jesus includes in this teaching the metaphor of the house, which is used often for both God and Satan (God's House=God's Kingdom). This could also be a reference back to King Ahaziah calling upon *Baal-zebub* in 2 Kings 1:2. More literally translated this could be "lord of the flies" or "lord of dung." Perhaps this gives you a little more insight to William Golding's 1954 novel *The Lord of the Flies.* The point Mark makes clear in this passage is that the religious leaders where projecting the idea that Jesus' abilities and powers were from Satan.

Verses 23-35 Jesus turns this verbal attack into one of His most important teachings about blasphemy. Blasphemy is usually defined as insulting or showing contempt to, by word or deed, a god, a religious person or thing, or sacred teachings. Interestingly, blasphemy is still considered a religious crime subject to the death penalty in over 30 countries today. In Jesus' day, speaking against or violating the many rules set up by the religious elite warranted the death penalty. Since the Jewish people were under Roman occupation they couldn't enforce the death penalty without the Roman governor's consent.

Jesus, on the other hand, teaches us that blasphemies can be forgiven. For Mark, speaking ill of Jesus and His ministry may indeed be blasphemy, but still open for forgiveness. As Jesus continues His teaching He cites one type of blasphemy as unforgiveable – an **eternal sin**. The unforgivable sin is blasphemy of the Holy Spirit. For Mark, as well as Matthew and Luke (Matthew 12:22-37, Luke 12:8-12) attributing the work of the Holy Spirit to Satan or vise versa is blasphemy and thus becomes unforgiveable.

Let me offer a word of caution for all Christian believers. A true believer in Jesus Christ as Lord and Savior of their life has the wonderful gift of being filled with the Holy Spirit. It seems most improbable that a believer would ever ascribe a movement of the Holy Spirit as somehow being of Satan. But I fear that the opposite might be an easy trap to fall into. Everything that has the appearance of being a movement of the Holy Spirit may not be.

The scriptures teach us to "test the spirits" (I John 4:1-6). Let's not quench or grieve the Holy Spirit, but let's also not be too hasty to attribute everything we see and experience as being from the Holy Spirit.

Verses 4:1-34 Jesus then **began to teach many things in parables.** Parables were a critical element in the teachings of Jesus. Initially there was a very large crowd but by verse 10 it is just Jesus and His disciples along with a few who were joined to the movement. Jesus explained that the use of parables was necessary so He could reveal the secrets (or mysteries) of the Kingdom of God. The parables were for insiders only, those "who had ears to hears." The outsiders, those who reject Jesus, would not have the spiritual ears to hear and understand. While Jesus' ministry would ultimately be to bring all persons unto Himself, these initial teachings were for His close followers.

Jesus At Odds:

1. Why would the religious leaders accuse Jesus of being possessed by Beelzebub?

2. What is your understanding of Jesus' teaching on blasphemy?

3. Were you offended by Jesus' remarks about His mother and brothers?

4. Why did Jesus resort to the use of parables in His teaching?

You At Odds:

1. Do you feel you have committed blasphemy? Has anyone you know?

2. Are you able to put God and His call on your life before your family?

3. How would you characterize yourself – rocky soil, thorns, or good soil?

NOTES

LESSON 5:

JESUS NOT YET REVEALED

READ: CHAPTER 4:35 THRU 6:6

Prayer: *Most powerful and yet most loving God, let us see You more clearly in the coming passages of scripture. Allow us a glimpse of Your glory that is revealed through Your Son Jesus. Allow us a special gift of understanding as we study these passages of Your Word. We thank You and praise You Father, in Jesus' name. AMEN.*

This extended passage serves two purposes. Mark gives us a split screen so to speak – a point and counter point. Mark's primary point is to show that Jesus is continuing His ministry of prophetic renewal for Israel even in the midst of clear opposition. The counter point Mark wants to convey is that Jesus' ministry is not limited to the Jewish people.

Verses 35-41 opens with Jesus taking His disciples to "the other side." The phrase is highly symbolic bringing to mind Moses parting the waters of the sea, Elijah crossing over the river, and God's people crossing over into the Promised Land. Here, however, it clearly showing Jesus crossing over into non-Jewish territory. The crossing itself was met with opposition, all be it a force of nature. A very prevalent belief in those days was a primordial evil lived beneath the sea. The disciples began to panic in the midst of the storm at sea, yet Jesus simply slept. When awaken and seeing the men's fear Jesus calmed the storm and rebuked the men for their lack of faith.

Verses 1-20 No sooner had they hit the other shore they were confronted with a man with an unclean spirit. This episode is one of Mark's most detailed and graphic. Once again Mark details for us the fact that the demons recognize Jesus immediately for who He was when every day men and women do not. *Son of the Most High God* is typically a Hellenistic term also found in the other Gospels.

Highlighted here is the fact that the man is possessed by, not one, but many unclean spirits collectively named *Legion*. Assuming the reference to be a Roman Legion because of their occupation of the region a legion would have been anywhere between 1000 and 5000 men. Because this area would have been an outpost and not an active battlefront we can assume the lower end of that scale. The text gives us a hint stating that the number of swine into which Jesus allowed the demons to indwell was about two thousand.

Swine were considered to be unclean by the Jewish community so the symbolism is not lost here. The unclean spirits were allowed to enter the unclean animals, which immediately stampeded into the sea (the dwelling place of evil) to their destruction. Jesus, a Jew, would certainly have been fully aware of this dynamic, but we need to be very careful not to cast this Pharisaical mindset to Jesus' motives.

As this episode comes to a close we see that the non-Jewish community as well as the religious leaders in Israel reject Jesus. The people saw the results of Jesus' power over a host of demons and were amazed. In this case, however, Jesus also disrupted their economy with the loss of 2000 swine. Not being a farmer or rancher I Googled it. Today's value of the herd would be over $300,000.

The man freed from demon possession was genuinely grateful and asked to follow Jesus. Jesus declined but directed the man to spread the good news of what the Lord had done for him. The now clean man began his own ministry of proclaiming Jesus to the *Decapolis*, an area of ten cities.

Verses 21-43 This section of scripture has often been called "A miracle on the way to a miracle." What we see is that once Jesus returns back across the sea His popularity is growing among the common people. A leader of the synagogue begs Jesus to heal his daughter. A leader of the synagogue is not normally a Scribe or Pharisee, but rather a local leader tasked with overseeing the community. But this is no small thing, as the religious leaders from Jerusalem will certainly confront him.

As the crowd joins Jesus and disciples on the way to heal the daughter, a woman who had a 12-year hemorrhage came close to Jesus in hopes of being healed. Her condition would have rendered her as unclean by Levitical Code. In her desperation (and certain embarrassment) she believed that if she could only touch Jesus' garments she would be healed.

When the woman did touch Jesus' clothes she was instantly healed, but significantly Jesus felt the transference of power. The text indicates that many people were touching Jesus in the push and shove of the crowd, but the healing power was transferred only to this woman. Jesus declared that is was her faith, not the touch or the clothes that made her well. We will come back to the woman in a moment.

In the time it took for this story line to unfold, the leader's daughter died. Messengers came to say it was over and Jesus didn't need to come. But Jesus had a greater plan. Taking only a few of His disciples and the parents Jesus went into the twelve-year-old little girl and brought her back to life.

Mark's symbolism is clear. The woman with a 12-year ailment, considered unclean and unable to have children represents the renewal of the old Israel and faith is the key ingredient. The young 12-year-old girl, just coming of age to be married and have children is raised to new life. She represents the new Israel that will emerge and grow under the power of the Son of God, the long awaited Messiah.

Verses 6:1-6a Mark brings us back to Jesus' hometown, which we are to assume is Nazareth. Jesus' family has been introduced as not being fully accepting of His ministry. The religious leadership has rejected Him and fear that He will disrupt their position within the Jewish community. The non-Jewish people have rejected Him in fear He will disrupt their economy. Now Jesus' own hometown reject Him.

Jesus At Odds:

1. Who or what is Jesus at odds with in the story of the man named Legion?

2. Why did the people ask Jesus to leave after casting out the demons?

3. What is your understanding of the story of the woman who touched Jesus?

4. Why did Jesus ask all the people to leave before He raises the girl from the dead?

You At Odds:

1. Has Jesus ever calmed a storm in your life?

2. How would the people of your community respond if Jesus cast out demons into pigs or livestock? Would they ask Him to leave?

3. Are people still being raised from the dead today?

NOTES

LESSON 6:

MINISTRY TO THE JEWS

READ: CHAPTER 6:6 THRU 7:23

Prayer: *Heavenly Father – As we continue to study and learn from Your scriptures help us to understand our calling and commission. Send us out into a world that is ripe for the harvest, yet resistant to hear and see. Lead us in righteousness and away from sinful pride and spiritual arrogance. As Your servants, let us remain near to the heart of Jesus. In His powerful name we pray. AMEN*

This section of scripture demonstrates malice and miracle, decadence and decency. While some the stories may be a simple recap of previous accounts, they are full of delicate truths.

Mark begins to paint a portrait of discipleship and mission.

Verses 6-13 is yet another commissioning scene but this time Jesus gives the disciples a mission under His personal authority with instructions on how to carry out their calling. Luke 10:1-16 gives a parallel version that is worth reading. The disciples are now the symbolic leaders of Israel's renewal.

Verses 14-16 Jesus' popularity now reaches Herod. Herod Antipas is the son of Herod the Great. He is appointed by Rome to rule over Galilee after the death of his father. While Herod was a Jew, he and his family were wealthy puppets of Rome. The entire family structure was incestuous. John the Baptizer confronted Herod and was imprisoned and executed. Once Jesus' popularity grew the rumor was that He was John the Baptist raised from the dead.

Verses 17-29 are the detailed past tense story of John the Baptizer's arrest and death. John calls Herod out on his decadent living and lands in jail. Herod's step daughter (and apparently niece) dances for the entertainment of Herod's guest. There are strong sexual innuendos in this scene. Herod is violating the taboos listed in Leviticus. One can only guess Herod's motives in offering the young girl half his kingdom. This would have certainly made her an attractive bargain in a possible marriage arrangement with one of the guests.

The girl runs to her mother for advice. Herodias, Herod's wife (and sister-in-law) apparently is as decadent as he is. She hated John for his interference and saw an opportunity for revenge. Herodias implicates her daughter in debauchery, telling her to ask for the head of John. Herod is by now drunk and unwilling to lose face in front of his guests, orders the execution.

Mark retells the story here because it shows the depth of unrighteousness Israel had fall to. It also obviously casts an ominous shadow over the renewal ministry of Jesus and His disciples. Jesus would later come before Herod after His arrest.

Verses 30-44 recount the miracle story of *Feeding the Five Thousand.* This wondrous event is recorded in each of the four gospels. Mark's placement of this story right after the death of John might seem strange at first, but only gives credence to the depth of unrighteousness of Herod. A lavish and decadent feast for the upper crust gives stark comparison to thousands of hungry people pressing in on Jesus and His disciples. In the absence of a true prophet or king to lead them the people are truly "sheep without a shepherd." This is a frequent Old Testament image.

The contrast doesn't stop there. Unlike the earthly king, Jesus had compassion on the people. With the extremely powerful and compelling portrait of the future Kingdom of God Jesus divides the five loaves and two fish and gives the bread and meat to the disciples to distribute. In Jesus' hands and with His blessing the division becomes a multiplication until all the people ate their fill. The portrait of the Kingdom of God is one where there will be no hunger or need for anyone. Jesus answered the prayers of the masses (and us) – "give us this day our daily bread."

The multiplication of the food and the twelve baskets of left-overs reminds us of the Old Testament Elijah and Elisha stories of feeding others during a famine. It is also a clear allusion to the restoration of Israel when the Messiah comes.

Verses 45-52 give us the story of the second crossing of the Sea of Galilee. Remember that the sea was considered the abode all sort of evil creatures giving rise to man's primordial fear. By the time Jesus had dismissed the crowd and took time to pray it was dark. The wind was blowing against the disciples in the boat and their fears were heightened. Seeing this Jesus came to them walking on the water. The disciples, in their terrified state thought He was a ghost, one of those evil creatures come up from the sea to pull them under.

Verse 50 is worth taking a little pause for. The scripture texts say that Jesus immediately spoke to the disciples. More than the immediacy, Jesus spoke words of comfort, *"Take heart, it is I, do not be afraid."* Literally, "it is I" in the Greek is *ego eimi.* This trans-lates "I AM," the name God gave for Himself when Moses had his burning bush encounter (Exodus 3:14). Mark is clearly equating Jesus with God. John puts this phrase in Jesus' words several times in his gospel account clearly outlining Jesus' Messiahship.

Verses 53-56 again demonstrate Jesus' popularity among the common people. Despite being asked to leave this non-Jewish area previously, people now are bringing their sick to be healed.

Verses 7:1-23 seem to make a quantum leap back into the realm of Jewish leadership but please remember that this lengthy section of scripture is about Jesus' ministry to the Jews. For Mark, the previous "crossing" is more of a review and summary of Jesus' power and popularity.

Human Traditions vs. God's Commandments: Once again Jesus encounters opposition from the Jewish leadership. Mark is clearly citing Jesus' newly found popularity as the reason for the opposition. As this story unfolds we see that the Pharisees and scribes resent having their authority put in question.

The story focuses on various purity codes established by the oral traditions of the Elders. These food preparation traditions are based on superfluous interpretations attached to the Law of Moses. Of course the interpretation and enforcement of the Law was under the sole authority of the religious elite. The Pharisees and scribes confronted Jesus, apparently in public, for not following the traditions of the elders – clearly translated as not honoring their authority.

Jesus responds with a strong indictment of His own by citing the prophet Isaiah. Reading the entire 29th chapter of Isaiah is a worthwhile homework assignment, but for now, Mark has Jesus zeroing in on the Septuagint version of verse 13. Jesus claims that the religious leaders have supplanted the commandments of God with their own human traditions. Jesus goes on to show how the Pharisees and scribes twisted the commandments to fill their own pockets.

Jesus then uses a little bawdy humor about what goes in and out of the human body to drive home His point. And the main point? It's what's inside that counts. It's what comes from the human heart that ultimately defiles someone, not failure to adhere to the traditions of men. Anytime rituals and rules become more important than the person of Jesus Christ and the Word of God then it becomes cultish. Take a moment to meditate on what Jesus is teaching in these verses:

» Major in spiritual renewal and minor in physical renewal.
» Major in the internal and minor in the external.
» Major in the moral and minor in the ceremonial.
» Major in people and minor in regulations.

Jesus At Odds:

1. What significance does the death of John the Baptist have for Jesus' ministry?

2. Do you sense any type of conflict in the story of the Feeding of the Five Thousand?

3. Explain the difference between commandments and traditions?

You At Odds:

1. Have you experienced a circumstance where others plotted against someone's ministry? How did you respond?

2. Do you believe in miracles? Have you ever experienced a miracle in your life?

3. Is the Church of today struggling with traditions of men verses God's directions?

NOTES

LESSON 7:

MINISTRY TO THE GENTILES

at odds with the world

READ: CHAPTER 7:24 THRU 8:9

Prayer: *Lord Jesus – In the power of Your Holy Spirit heal our minds and hearts of all selfishness and pride. Open our eyes and our ears to the needs of others around, and not just those who are like us. Move us out of self-created zones we've built to protect ourselves and into the world that needs us to share our faith in You. You are our Lord and our Savior. Hear our prayers! AMEN*

Verses 7:24 – 8:9 remind us that Mark's literary style is not marked by chapter and verse, or even strict chronological order, but by ministry segments. Here, Jesus unceremoniously moves from teaching (and confronting) the folks of His own religious background to performing miracles on behalf of Gentiles. These are people whom the religious elite would have little or nothing to do with. Yet here is Jesus healing these marginalize people.

Syrophoenician Woman: Jesus moves north out of Galilee in an apparent effort to be alone and away from the constant antagonism of the Jewish leaders. Unfortunately, good news travels fast and Jesus is unable to *escape notice*. A woman, who Mark makes sure we know is not Jewish, bowed down at Jesus' feet begging Him to rid her daughter of an unclean spirit. While some commentators would disagree I think Mark is making the point that the woman was also biracial. She was of Syrian and Phoenician background. Mark is letting the reader know that this person is just about as low as you can get. A good Jewish religious leader would have little to do with a gentile. Worse yet, a woman! Add to that a woman with mixed personal history! And yet Jesus was willing to break all the rules of social etiquette to minister to this woman.

At first glance, Jesus' reply might shock us. It appears that Jesus insults the woman by calling her a dog! There are some hints here that tell us otherwise. Jesus' fame follows Him. This woman has heard the stories of Jesus healing people and casting outs demons. She believes that Jesus can do the same for her daughter. Instead of speaking to the woman about healing and demons, Jesus speaks to her about feeding children, softening the rhetoric. Pious Jews did often call gentiles "dogs." Jesus, however, uses a term better translated, "puppy" or pet. There is nothing derogatory in the word.

The majority of commentators do believe that Jesus is stating that His mission is to the people of Israel first, but Mark is showing us the depth of love and compassion Jesus has for all people regardless of their personal heritage and social status.

The woman shows boldness of faith in coming to Jesus and bowing before Him, but she shows her humility and meekness in her response. *"Lord, even the dogs under the table eat the children's crumbs."* The woman's faith that Jesus could cast out her daughter's demons was so strong that she believed even the tiniest bit of left over power would result in a miracle.

Healing a Deaf Man: Jesus is still in Gentile territory. Healing a non-Jewish man who is both deaf and has a speech impediment sends a strong message that the Kingdom of God will extend beyond the Jewish nation. Restoration and renewal will come to all those who believe in Jesus as the Messiah.

As before, Jesus healed the man in private and ordered those with him to tell no one. This is yet another example of Mark detailing what is called the Messianic Secret. But, as before, those immediately involved in the healing proclaimed Jesus and the healing all the more.

Feeding of the Four Thousand: Many commentators consider this a retelling of the previous story, however, the details are have significance in their difference. Probably of most significance is that Mark's first feeding miracle was offered to the people of Israel. This feeding miracle is offered to Gentiles. Instead of twelve leftover baskets, clearly symbolic of Israel, there were seven leftover baskets, symbolizing those nationalities outside the nation of Israel.

This section of Jesus' ministry to the Gentiles, despite His insistence that He was sent to the children of Israel, gives credibility and authority for the disciples and Paul to expand their mission. It also gives today's Christians the divine example of their Lord and confidence to fulfill the Great Commission.

Jesus At Odds:

1. Do you think Jesus' ministry to non-Jewish people caused trouble for Him?

2. Why did Jesus repeatedly tell folks not to tell others about His miracles?

3. How does the feeding compare or contrast with the feeding of the 5000?

You At Odds:

1. How much time do you think your pastor should spend ministering to people who are not a member of your congregation?

2. Are the members of your congregation genuinely excited about their ministry to the community around them?

3. Do you sometimes doubt that Jesus can really supply all your needs?

LESSON 8:

JESUS
REVEALED

READ: CHAPTER 8:10 THRU 9:29

Prayer: *Most Gracious Father – there are so many things we don't know, so many things that are mysteries yet unsolved. Give us fresh visions of Your Son. Help us to know who Jesus really is. Guide us in these visions so we might live for Him and for You. Hear our prayers in the name of Jesus. AMEN.*

This lengthy section of scriptures begins the process of re-vealing the real Jesus. Again, Mark is not concerned with precise chronological details but does want for his readers to discover who Jesus really is. Ultimately this is the purpose behind Mark's gospel account, to introduce the Son of God who ushers in the Kingdom of God.

Verses 10-12 have Jesus and His disciples returning to Galilee via a boat to a place called Dalmanutha. This is believed to be a location on the shore between Capernaum and Magdala. The Pharisees were apparently waiting for Jesus to strike up another ar-gument. They had obviously heard about the miraculous feedings, the healings and the casting out of unclean spirits. They pressed Jesus for a sign, but discerning their motive, Jesus refused.

Interestingly, Jesus down plays His miracles and never flaunts them as demonstrations of His power. He could have easily given these Pharisee a sign but Jesus knew it would not lead to faithful acceptance of Him. If you journey through the gospel account of Jesus' ministry, you see He repeatedly refused to perform signs when demanded of Him. Jesus criticized those who missed the point of His miracles and based their faith solely on signs. Mark will record Jesus' triumphal entry into Jerusalem later in chapter 11. John's gospel account of this messianic demonstration suggests that many in the crowd were not there to celebrate the arrival of the Messiah, but only to see signs and wonders. Modern day sign chasers would be no more respected by Jesus than those of His day.

Verses 13-21. After this brief altercation with the Pharisee Jesus gets back into the boat and went *across to the other side.* Crossing over always holds a deep eschatological context but here it is a simple device to get away from the Pharisees. Apparently, they didn't go but a little further along the northern shore of the Sea of Galilee to Bethsaida.

While in the boat the disciples discover they forgot to restock their bread. Jesus uses this as a teaching moment warning the disciples to *beware of the yeast of the Pharisee.* Jesus was simply telling them to be careful not to fall into the trap of legalism, quarreling, and pride. This is a great message for any congregation, but the disciples didn't get it. They were focused on not having enough bread. Mark wants us to understand that the disciples were still blind and deaf to Jesus' miracles and teachings.

Verses 22-26. Mark continues the theme of blindness. Some people brought a blind man to Jesus to be healed. Once again Jesus moves to a place of privacy. Interestingly, almost comical, Mark tells how the blind man receives partial sight, undoubtedly mocking the disciples for their continued partial blindness. But Jesus is persistent and the man regains full sight.

Verses 27-33 bring us the story of Jesus' first self-revealing declaration. He and His disciples had journeyed to the northern most part of what had formally belonged to Israel. As they went Jesus asked the disciples, *Who do people say that I am?* Not unexpectedly, their answers identified Jesus as being associated with John the Baptist, Elijah, or other prophets. But Jesus then put His disciples on the spot, *But who do you say that I am?*

We shouldn't be surprised that Peter was the one to speak up, but perhaps a little amazed that none of the other disciples did. Significantly, Peter proclaims Jesus to be the Christ, the Messiah. Jesus, without any correction or disclaimer, orders them to tell no one.

Jesus, referencing Himself, then states that the Son of Man (often used as alternate title for the future Messiah) must be rejected by the religious leaders, killed, and three days later rise again. This is first of three declarations where Jesus would speak plainly about His pending future.

The impetuous Peter takes Him aside and reprimands Jesus for His declaration. This takes us immediately back to the "partial blindness" of the disciples. Despite Peter's faith affirmation that Jesus is the Messiah just moments before, he clearly does not understand what the role of the long awaited Messiah is and still does not understand the positional relationship one must have with his Lord and Savior.

Jesus in turn rebukes Peter in what has become one of the most popular quotes in today's church. *Get behind me, Satan!* Jesus' reprimand is the same as He gave to the Pharisees and scribes — having concern over human things verses divine things. Peter, like the religious leaders, was concerned over earthly human kingdoms and not the Kingdom of God.

Verses 34-9:1. You may be beginning to see that Mark is very adept at sequencing his stories using various themes. These verses are no exception. As Peter demonstrates his misunderstanding of his positional relationship with Jesus, Mark immediately follows with Jesus' teaching on what it means to be His disciple.

Jesus rather pointedly teaches that to be His disciple you must deny yourself (which Peter did not), take up your cross (which Peter rebuked Jesus for mentioning), and follow me (which Peter almost failed in the courtyard). The phrase about taking up your cross is an indication or foreshadowing that Jesus knew how He was to die. Jesus follows with the cost of discipleship using little turns of a phrase.

Jesus ends His teaching with one of the most debated verses in scripture. Jesus boldly proclaims that some present at that moment will not experience death without witnessing the coming of the Kingdom of God. What did Jesus mean? Matthew, Luke, and Mark follow this saying with the Transfiguration of Jesus (Matthew 17:1-8; Mark 9:2-8, Luke 9:28-36) of which Peter, James and John witnessed. Several present at the time would have witnessed the Crucifixion and experience the post Resurrection Jesus. Others would have witnessed the unprecedented expansion of Christianity after the Resurrection. Any or all of these events may be the basis for Jesus' statement.

Verses 2-8 The Transfiguration of Jesus is found in Matthew and Luke, but not in John's gospel account, oddly so in that John is more otherworldly in his understanding of who Jesus was and is. There are a host of explanations of what the Transfiguration is all about ranging from proof that Jesus was an alien from outer space (Von Daniken), to the passing of divine power from God.

Little can be offered to the conversation about this dazzling mystical event. The happening is not all that unlike the mountain setting with Moses and the elders (Exodus 24). It also served for the disciples as a ratification of what role Jesus was to have in the restoration of Israel. Jesus appeared in stunning white display with Moses, the founding father of Israel, and Elijah, the visionary prophet who restored Israel.

Notably, the disciples present didn't know what to do or how to respond to this transformation of their leader. Also remarkable, Peter addresses Jesus as "Rabbi" during this rather mystical event when earlier he boldly stated that Jesus was "messiah" or "the Christ." Peter, perhaps as representative of all the disciples, seems to wavier in his understanding of Who Jesus really is. One would think after witnessing the Transfiguration and hearing the voice from heaven the disciples present would be even firmer in their faith.

Verses 9 – 13: Once again Jesus orders the disciples to keep quiet about what they've just seen. As might be expected, however, the subject of Elijah's return came up. How could "The Son of Man" be risen from the dead before Elijah returns. The disciples were still tied up in the Scribes and Pharisee's teachings. Was this transfiguration of Moses and Elijah with Jesus to be interpreted as Elijah's return? The disciples just didn't understand. Jesus clearly states that Elijah has come in the person of John. John isn't Elijah, but he came with the same message of repentance and restoration.

Verse 14-29: While Matthew and Luke seem to have parallels to this story, Mark's version is uncharacteristically more detailed. This may be the result of having a closer association with the story or a later redaction. Whatever the case may be, we see the reoccurring theme of arguments with the scribes and Jesus' popularity. More importantly, we see that the disciples are actively engaging in Jesus' ministry but unable to manifest the same power. Jesus uses the event to reiterate His teaching that faith and miracles go hand in hand and signs, in and of themselves, are not what are most important.

Jesus At Odds:

1. Why did Jesus feel it was necessary to warn the disciples about the Pharisees?

2. What do you think of Peter in this section of scripture? Good parts? Not so Good?

3. Why did Peter want to build three booths or shelters? To honor or to memorialize?

4. How did the disciples respond when unable to cast out an evil spirit?

You At Odds:

1. Did you ever feel like rebuking Jesus for something happening in your life?

2. What was your most recent mountain top experience? How do you feel now?

3. Do you feel your church struggles to keep up the ministry of Jesus? If so, why?

NOTES

LESSON 9:

Jesus Style Discipleship

Read: Chapter 9:30 thru 50

Prayer: *Precious Jesus – We worship You and praise Your holy name. We read of You taking little children into Your arms. We would love nothing more than to be gathered into Your arms. But You've called us to reach out to others. Help us to be Your disciples, bringing children of all ages to You. Embrace us all with Your grace and peace. Hear our prayer. AMEN.*

Verses 30 – 41: This section of scripture has Jesus and the disciples passing through Galilee. It is not clear if Jesus doesn't want anyone to know He is passing through Galilee or if He doesn't want people to know about the events of the Transfiguration and the casting out of demons. The way many translation record this verse, it appears that Jesus doesn't wish for anyone but His disciples to hear the second announcement concerning the events of His death. Whichever it might be, Mark is clearly continuing the Messianic Secret theme.

What must have been heartbreaking for Jesus, the disciples were arguing among themselves "who was the greatest." When Jesus asked, the disciples were embarrassed and silent, but He knew, prompting Him to offer what has been dubbed a parable of reversal. There are many of these throughout the gospels (e.g. "Whoever wants to be first must be last").

As His own example, Jesus places a little child before them. A little child would be considered the least or last within the family or household. A true disciple of Jesus would not argue over who was the greatest, but would humble themselves to welcome one of the least.

The disciples discover someone casting out demons in Jesus' name and tried to stop them. Jesus admonishes them not to hinder the person's ministry and then launches into a strong teaching. Since it is highly unlikely Jesus would advocate cutting off one's own hand or foot, or plucking out one's own eye something else must be at play here. In order to catch the full impact we must do a quick review of the last sequence of events:

1. Jesus is Transfigured but only a small group of disciples witness the event.
2. Coming down off the mountain the remaining disciples were arguing with the scribes after being unable to cast out demons. Jesus takes care of the matter personally.
3. The next scene has the disciples arguing among themselves over who was the greatest. Jesus teaches about humility and suggesting greatness was found in being the least.
4. The disciples respond by tell Jesus someone else was casting out demons in His name (while they were yet unable to) and they tried to stop them.

While telling the disciples not to hinder someone else's ministry Jesus brings back the theme of the little child. Hindering or causing someone to stumble was unacceptable and punishable. The disciples were still all wrapped up in their own importance. Their stumbling block was pride! The hand, foot, and eye are all metaphors for pride. Pride in a disciple can become a millstone that drags you to the bottom of the sea or casts you into a fiery hell. Pride within a disciple is paramount to salt loosing its taste – good for nothing (Matthew 5:13).

Jesus At Odds:

1. Jesus repeatedly told the disciples that He would be betrayed and killed, yet the disciples failed to understand. Why couldn't they get it?

2. The disciples argued among themselves as to who was the greatest. What were they up against or at odds with here?

3. How do you think the disciples felt when Jesus put a little child in front of them?

You At Odds:

1. Do you sense there are arguments in the church over who is the greatest? How do these arguments manifest themselves?

2. Have you sometimes resented the ministry of someone else who wasn't part of the appointed team?

3. Have you lost your saltiness? What does that mean? How do you get it back?

NOTES

LESSON 10:

Judea to Jerusalem

Read: Chapter 10:1 thru 52

Prayer: *Most Powerful yet Loving God — We stand in awe of Your majesty yet are amazed at the depth of Your grace and love. With Your power and strength draw us into Your Kingdom. With Your love teach us how to live in such a way that others are drawn to Your Son and into Your Kingdom as well. All glory belongs to You! In Jesus' name, hear our prayer. AMEN.*

At times Mark's purpose and design in his gospel structure is clear and usually concise. But this chapter creates a quandary. Mark rarely appears to be concerned about chronological correctness but this section is clearly showing Jesus moving toward Jerusalem where He will confront the establishment and their institutions. Yet, this section of scripture also addresses Kingdom relationships within the family and within the social-economic-political world.

Verses 1-16: As Jesus moves back into Judea, He is confronted by the Pharisees again. While we aren't given the context of how the subject came up, the Pharisees challenge Jesus on the issue of divorce. Jesus contends that Moses established the rules of divorce only because of their "hardness of heart." Jesus insists that relationship regulations between men and women go back further than Moses all the way to creation. Again, we can hear echoes of Jesus' teaching God's rules, not man's.

The Pharisees understood divorce as a male privilege or right, but Jesus clearly believes women have the same entitlement. However, Jesus moves the whole question of divorce into a matter of adultery. Without a doubt the establishment of divorce laws were designed to circumvent the commandment against adultery. (See Deuteronomy 24:1-4, Jeremiah 3:8)

Wanting always to err on the side of grace, divorce and adultery should be handled much in the same way that Jesus addressed it when the Pharisees brought before Him a woman caught in the act of adultery (John 8:3-11). I'm not sure what readers today should make of the fact that many scholars insist that this section of John's gospel was not part of the original manuscript. My humble advice on this difficult issue is "may grace abound" (Romans 6:1-3).

Verse 17 – 31: When approached by an apparently pious man, Jesus uses the encounter to teach the relationship between worldly wealth and "treasure in heaven." Uncharacteristically Mark introduced the man as one not trying to argue and debate, but genuinely seeking guidance from Jesus. Surprisingly, Jesus responds rather callously giving a synopsis of the Ten Commandments. The man confessed to having kept the commandments since youth and the obvious truth of his confession caused Jesus to be moved with love. Jesus sensed, however, that the man had one thing holding him back from being a true follower.

Whether or not Jesus actually intended for the man to give all his possessions away, He was making it clear that nothing can stand in the way of full commitment. The man was shocked at Jesus' declaration and was unable to give up the one thing that stood between him and true discipleship.

Jesus did not disqualify the wealthy from entering the Kingdom, but acknowledged how hard it is to give up the comfort and status of wealth for trusting God in all things. Not surprisingly, the disciples didn't understand. They still held on to worldly concepts of success and accomplishment – none of which would gain access to the Kingdom.

Jesus spoke clearly that men and women cannot save themselves regardless of worldly wealth and status. Just as clearly Jesus declared that God can accomplish all things – even those that are impossible for men and women.

Of course Peter felt compelled to compare himself to the rich man who sadly walked away. "We have left everything to follow you." Jesus gave (what may be redacted) a promise that all things would be restored to those who sacrifice for the Kingdom. Jesus qualified His promise with a parable of reversal – restoration may not come in the way we think.

Verses 32 – 45: In Jesus' teaching we are moved from a Kingdom understanding of Marriage to a Kingdom knowledge of wealth, and now to a Kingdom awareness of sociopolitical status. As the disciples continued their journey toward Jerusalem Jesus pulled them aside and told them again for the third time that He would be killed and then rise again on the third day. Mark offers a few more details on how the events would unfold.

As a clear indication that some of the disciples still didn't understand or that they simply were not listening, James and John asked Jesus a question that we would find totally incomprehensible. "Teacher (*not Lord or Master*⁵), we want you to do for us whatever we ask of you." Wow! Jesus plays along asking what it is they wanted. James and John asked that Jesus grant them the highest seats of honor when He is glorified. Wow again!

Can you imagine the hurt, not to mention the frustration Jesus must have felt? Nevertheless, Jesus spelled it out for them clearly as they obviously had no clue what was just ahead for them all. As to the brothers' place in glory, Jesus stated that wasn't His call, but they would share in a death like His. The remaining ten disciples became angry with James and John. It's not made clear if they were mad because the brothers broke Jesus' heart or because they were pushing in ahead of the others for the best seats in glory. You might guess the latter because Jesus followed with yet another

---

5 *Emphasis Mine*

parable of reversal – those who wish to be great or first must take the role of a servant.

Verses 46 – 52: Mark follows with the story of Blind Bartimaeus. While both Matthew and Luke record this story, Mark's placement here is painfully obvious. The disciples have been following Jesus but are still blind to Who Jesus really is. A totally blind man, however, knows instinctively Who Jesus is. The give away here is the question Jesus asks Bartimaeus. It is exactly the same question Jesus asked the disciples when they pridefully asked to have the best seats of honor. "What do you want me to do for you?" In a reversal of the disciples, once Bartimaeus' eyesight is restored he becomes a true follower of Jesus. Again, Jesus confirms that faith is the basis behind miracles.

Jesus At Odds:

1. The Pharisees questioned Jesus about divorce. What were they trying to do?

2. What did Jesus mean when He said the Kingdom belongs to the children? How would the religious leaders have taken that remark?

3. Jesus said it was hard for the rich to enter the Kingdom of God. What did He mean?

4. Jesus asked some of His disciples if they could drink the cup that He would drink. How did that question fit the disciples' request to have the seats of honor once Jesus came into His glory?

You At Odds:

1. Have you ever sought after or watched others seek after the places of honor within the church? What happened and how did you feel?

2. Do you think you are rich in Jesus' eyes?

3. If you could teach your children something from this section of scripture, what would it be?

NOTES

LESSON 11:

THE CONFLICT INTENSIFIES

READ: CHAPTER 11:1 THRU 26

Prayer: *Heavenly Father – Sometimes the plain word of Your scriptures are hard for us to understand. In the power and presence of Your Holy Spirit help us to look beyond our limited knowledge to the depth of truth You have laid out before us. Show us the promise, moving us away from the puzzle that we've created within our own understanding. Let us learn and live the principles You have offered for us. Hear our prayer. AMEN.*

This chapter records Mark's description of the last week of Jesus' life on earth. This section starts with what appears as a triumphal entry but rapidly turns into intense conflict ultimately leading to the crucifixion of the Son of God.

Verses 1-11. Unlike Matthew and Luke, Mark records the event we now call Palm Sunday with little fanfare. John gives his own version of the story as well. Mark just gives you the facts and moves on. The facts, however, are important. Jesus creates a living portrait of the prophesy foretold in Zech 9:9. Zechariah's version tells of the triumphant entry of a new ruler who will restore Israel and bring lasting peace. The people misunderstood the prophecy as promising a political reinstatement of Israel's place in the world.

Jesus, in dramatizing the prophecy, received the same misunderstanding. People came out shouting praises. They began waving palm branches and laying their coats in His path, all symbols of honor and acceptance. They shouted *Hosanna,* which originally was used as a chant or prayer to God, "O Save!" By Jesus' day it was a shout of acclamation and approval. Riding on a lowly ass, Jesus symbolized His humility rather than some type of victory parade. The result was more controversy with the religious leaders and the praises and adulations soon turned into jeers and flogging.

Verses 12-14. This section of scripture is difficult to understand. There are numerous commentaries giving just as numerous reasons why Jesus would curse a fig tree. Here are some thoughts to consider as you try to understand this passage.

Mark has placed the cursing of the fig tree before and after the cleansing of the temple. It would seem that the meaning of the event is connected to what happened in the temple which will be discussed a little bit later, but for now Jesus declared the temple a house of prayer, not a den of robbers.

Another clue Mark gives us is the location from which Jesus came into Jerusalem. Verse 11:1 says that they came from Bethphage and Bethany at the Mount of Olives, both of which are to the east of the city. Bethphage is literally translated as "house of unripe figs." The name of the area has a long history. Shortening that history for you, many believe that the fruit that tempted Adam and Eve was a fig (not an apple!). The name Bethphage was given as a place of unripe figs so that one might not be tempted to pick them and thus fall to the sins of Adam and Eve. More to the point, this was an area where figs where grown and harvested. Also noteworthy, figs generally were harvested after Passover, which was one week away. Also of importance, figs normally began to show up on the trees prior to the tree coming into full leaf.

Verse 13 has the strange phrase "because it was not the season for figs." Many commentators believe this means it was not harvest time, which didn't begin for another week. Putting what we know into play, Jesus would have normally expected to find figs on the tree, but did not.

Verses 15 – 19. All four Gospels record the story of Jesus cleansing the temple, though Mark's version is the most basic. What is behind Jesus' actions is the fact that the temple officials were running a money exchange. Only temple money could be used to buy animals and birds to be used for sacrifices. Pilgrims coming into Jerusalem for Passover would bring their sacrifices to the temple for inspection. If found unsatisfactory, which was very likely after a long journey, the pilgrims would need to buy a sacrificial animal sold by temple officials. Add to this scandal, the pilgrims were being charged a high rate of exchange for the temple currency. Jesus ran the moneychangers and the merchants selling sacrificial animals out of the temple proclaiming the temple as a house of prayer. This event was, for Mark, the beginning of the Chief Priests and scribes schemes to kill Jesus.

Verses 20 – 26. The next day Jesus and the disciples were passing by the same way and encountered the cursed fig tree. Seeing that the tree had withered and died Peter pointed it out as a way of asking why. Jesus turned the experience into a lesson on prayer. First and foremost this entire section is about the importance and power of prayer. Equally as important, however, is the possibility that Jesus was demonstrating how totally unfruitful the temple officials were and thus their end was destructions. Even deeper in meaning, the Chief Priests and scribes plans to kill Jesus would only result in their own eternal death.

Jesus At Odds:

1. As Jesus entered into the city on a donkey how did the crowd respond? How did the religious leaders respond?

2. Why did Jesus put a curse on the fig tree? What implications might it have to the other scenes in this section of scripture?

3. What or who was Jesus at odds with when He cleared out the temple?

You At Odds:

1. What was your first reaction to Jesus cursing the fig tree? Did you change your feelings after reading how Jesus responded the next day?

2. How would you feel if people set up a yard sale inside the sanctuary?

3. How do you respond to abuses or degrading behavior in the church?

4. Do you feel Jesus is calling you to restore genuine ministry. Do you feel you have Jesus' authority to do so?

NOTES

LESSON 12:

CONFLICT WITH THE SANHEDRIN

READ: CHAPTER 11:27 THRU 12:44

Prayer: *Most High God – Thank You for watching over us and guiding us. Continue to lead us away from those who would deceive us and trick us with their false teachings. In the power of Your Holy Spirit give us the gift of discernment that we might recognize Your teachings and live by their truths. Receive our prayer in Jesus name. AMEN.*

This lengthy section records several attempts by the elite members of the religious leadership to trap Jesus into saying or doing something wrong. Each time Jesus is not fooled by their wiles and turns the encounters into teaching moments. As Jesus returns to the temple, apparently the first time since casting out the money-changers, the conflict begins.

Verses 27 – 33. As Jesus reenters the temple area a group of religious leaders, including the chief priest surround Him. They challenge His authority to disrupt the normal business of the temple and ask who gave Him such authority. In an interesting turnabout Jesus cross-examines their presumed authority by asking was John's baptism of God or of men. Out of fear of the gathered crowd's reaction they answered truthfully that they didn't know. They didn't know because God had given them neither the gifts nor authority to judge over such matters. Jesus then declined to answer their question regarding His authority because they obviously lacked the God given gift of discernment to understand that His authority was from above.

Verses 1 – 12: Jesus then told them the Parable of the Vineyard, which is also shared with Matthew and Luke. In Aristotelian Greek understanding parables have been defined as having only one point. This has been a terrible limiting perspective brought right into our own age. This viewpoint says ignore all other details and similes and search for the one main truth. This particular parable demonstrates precisely why we should not limit ourselves to the Aristotelian definition.

The parable is a painfully clear portrait of the nation of Israel. God sent prophet after prophet to restore Israel into a fruitful people (and nation), but each was ignored, even killed. In the parable God sends His only Son and prophetically Jesus says He too will be killed. The similitude is unmistakable. The great truth comes in the form of a Q&A, "What will the owner of the vineyard do?" Jesus' emphatic answer is God will destroy the tenants and give the vineyard to others.

The religious leaders tried to arrest Jesus, but could not because of the crowd. They left Him alone waiting for another opportunity.

Verses 13 – 17. Again the Pharisees came to entrap Jesus. This time they brought Herodians with them. Herodians were for the most part Jews who politically favored Herod, a puppet leader put in place by the Romans. Herod was corrupt and violated many of the religious taboos of the Jews.

The question placed before Jesus was whether it was lawful under Jewish law to pay taxes to Caesar. If Jesus had said no, the Herodians would immediately report Him to the Romans. If Jesus had said yes, He would have been in disfavor with the people. Just as important, the Pharisees would have attacked Him again over His actions of chasing out the moneychangers from the temple and overturning their tables. Their money exchange was so Jews wouldn't have to use Roman coinage to pay for their sacrifices.

Jesus again turns the table on the group. Asking the Pharisees and Herodians to produce a denarius, they did. At least one in the group had violated Jewish law by having in their possession a graven image. It would not have been surprising for a Herodian to have such a coin, but it put the Pharisees in "unclean" company. As a side note, Pilot went to great lengths to appease the Jews by not having engraved images or inscriptions on his coinage. The particular coin produced apparently had Caesar's image and came from outside the area of Pilot's influence.

Jesus' reply is one of the most quoted verses in the Bible often missing or overlooking the main point. The point has nothing to do with paying taxes. It is all about loyalties. The Pharisees loyalties were obviously not to God.

Verses 18-27. The next group of religious leaders to test Jesus was the Sadducees. These were members of a second group of Jewish religious leaders. The Sadducees tended to be wealthy while the Pharisees were considered to be more middle class. Theologically, the two groups differed in several ways. The most notable difference centered on the resurrection and the belief in spirits and angels. The Pharisees accepted an understanding of the resurrection of the soul but not a physical resurrection. The Pharisees also believed in the presences of evils spirits and the existence of angels. The Sadducees believed in neither. For them there was neither reward nor punishment after death.

The question the Sadducees asked Jesus went beyond testing Him. They were clearly mocking Him posing a theological joke. Jesus would have, of course, known their beliefs. He started with a mild reprimand, "you know neither the scriptures nor the power of God [*my translation*]." If we'd been there, I'm sure we would have heard an audible gasp from the crowd.

First, Jesus acknowledged the reality of the resurrection but counters the joke with the teaching that those rising from the dead will be like angels in heaven, not marrying each other as they do on earth. This leaves the debate of a physical resurrection unanswered. Secondly, Jesus uses scripture (Exodus 3:6) to solidify the reality of the resurrection citing that God was not the God of the dead, but of the living.

Verses 28-34: In what would seem like an ironic twist one of the scribes come to Jesus' rescue. The Sadducees and the Scribes would have very little love loss, as they were opponents theologically. The Scribes primary function was to give legal interpretation to the Law and scriptures. The Sadducees totally rejected any man made expansion of the Law. One might see a little one-up-manship going on here. There is, however, something a little deeper. Some of the religious elite where truly seeking after God and began to see Jesus for who He really was. The Scribe asked Jesus which was the first commandment. As might be expected Jesus recited Deuteronomy 6:5 which is the first of the commandments. Surprisingly, however, Jesus didn't stop. He continued by adding a verse from Leviticus 19:18.

If the Scribe truly was trying to trip Jesus up, here was the opening. On the surface Jesus had answered the question incorrectly. But a discerning heart sees beyond the literal and the legal. Loving God and loving others are so tightly entwined that they form the core of what God expects of His people. While the Scribe confirmed that Jesus had answered well, you have to smile. The Scribe did respond with a touch of one-up-manship by adding that loving God and loving your neighbor was better than burnt offerings and sacrifices (Micah 6:6-8).

Verses: 35-37. These three verses actually relate back to the encounter with the Sadducees over the reality of the resurrection. Jesus left that debate with the words that our God is the God of the living. With a little depth of logic Jesus asks how the Christ can be the son of David when David calls Him my Lord. If the Christ has yet to come, then He is the Lord of David after his death – yet ours is the God of the living. David unknowingly confirms a belief in life after death. David's declaration in Psalm 110 is actually saying that it is the Lord who calls him to the throne and to the position of king.

But deeper still Mark places in Jesus' teaching the evidence of the pre-existence of Christ. There are stories throughout the Old Testament of the presence of Christ. In the New Testament John's gospel begins with the firm affirmation that the Christ (the Word) was with God and was God from the beginning. Here Jesus confirms that the Christ cannot be both the Lord and son of David unless the Christ was pre-existent from the beginning.

The passage ends with acclamation of the crowd for Jesus' teaching. Is the reception of His teaching because they are hearing the true Word of God or because Jesus is doing a great job of putting the religious leaders in their place?

Verses: 38-44. These verses start with an unexpected warning to beware of the Scribes. Jesus had just affirmed a Scribe as being not far from the Kingdom. Yet, we shouldn't be too surprised because the overwhelming majority of the religious leaders were plotting Jesus' death.

Two stories are woven together with the word "widow." If nothing else, the Scribes were being contrasted with the widows. Scribes were notorious for wearing long (often expensive) robes setting themselves apart from the average working person. As is often the case today in certain circles, the Scribes expected and enjoyed being honored with lofty recognition and prestigious seating in the synagogues and at banquets. Jesus was saying they were pompous and prideful. In contrast, the widow is demure and humble.

The accusation that the Scribes were devouring widows' houses is unclear. Was Jesus citing a specific instance or was He highlighting a common practice? What we do know is that the Scribes offered many services to the people. They would offer legal advice and financial guidance, even at times mediating when deals or exchanges were made. However, the Scribes were restricted from accepting payment for their services. They could, on the other hand, solicit donations in support of their religious profession. Again, it is not clear if Jesus was referring to a Scribe giving poor or even corrupt advice to a widow, or if He was referring to the Scribes soliciting donations from the vulnerable widows.

The second story does give us a possible hint to what Jesus was referring to. Jesus is clearly showing the distinctive difference between the poor widow and the rich, of which the religious leaders

would have been included. Every Jewish family was required to give
offerings and sacrifices to the Lord. The Scribes are the ones who
determined what was an acceptable gift. In their so-called wisdom
the Scribes declared that two copper coins was the smallest gift
allowed. The copper coin (lepton) was of little value much as the
penny is of little value today. For the widow in our story, two such
coins were all she had.

The treasury in the temple was one of the rooms just off the
portico. The people would come to the treasury to offer their gifts
for use in the temple. History books tell us that the treasury was
a large chest or box, perhaps even several boxes. There is some
indication that there were as many as 13 boxes, one for each
tribe and one strictly for the temple. These boxes had trumpet
shaped horns or funnels in which the money was placed. The
custom was for one of the temple officials to stand watch by the
treasury to monitor and approve the gifts that were being offered.
The giver was required to announce out loud the amount and the
purpose of the gift.

Again, it is not clear if this type of oppressiveness was what
Jesus was referring to, but Jesus did declare the widow's gift to
be greater than all the other gifts given that day. Jesus could have
easily been saying that the Scribe's rules were stripping the widows
of all they had. The widow truly wanted to give to the Lord, but
the requirements set by the Scribes for a minimum gift "devoured"
her total living.

Jesus At Odds:

1. What was Jesus thinking about when He told the Parable of the Tenants?

2. The religious leaders were really putting Jesus to the test. What was their true motive and how did Jesus handle the situation?

3. What was Jesus at odds with in the story of the Widow's Offering?

You At Odds:

1. What subject is guaranteed to spark a debate in your Sunday School class? What is the motive behind bring up that subject?

2. Has your church and congregation been "good tenants" of the Good News?

3. How would you categorize your giving to the Lord through the church?

NOTES

LESSON 13:

TRIBULATION AND TRIUMPH

READ: CHAPTER 13:1-37

Prayer: *Lord Jesus, Son of the Most High God – We are so anxious for Your coming. Our hearts yearn for Your victorious return. But, we also know that suffering, pain and many trials will come first. We already are facing them. Help us, in the power of Your Holy Spirit, to be watchful and alert. Strengthen us that we might stand firm in the face of the coming ordeals. Let us not falter. You are our Lord, our Savior, as well as our Friend in times of need. Receive our prayer in Your most powerful name. AMEN*

This entire chapter is one piece, a prophetic pronouncement by Jesus. I use the word "pronouncement" purposefully. Despite the ominous and dark future Jesus outlines, it is held together by the positive and powerful promise of Jesus' victorious return.

Verses: 1-2. It is so easy to miss what is happening in these two verses. Jesus cautions His listeners about the Scribes and how they coerce people, even poor widows, into giving to their personal support and to the temple. Jesus then praises a poor woman's two mites as the greatest gift of the day.

Herod began remodeling of the temple in 19 BC. Even now under Herod's son, the temple was not complete and would not be complete until 63 AD. As Jesus and the disciples were leaving the temple, one of them brings attention to the wonderful edifice they've just left. The temple was beautiful ... and it takes a lot of *money* to build and maintain such a wonderful complex ... all to the glory of God! The disciple was giving justification, even if unknowingly, for the strong-arm tactics to raise money. Jesus immediately responded that this beautiful temple would soon be destroyed and indirectly He was saying all the money spent would have been for nothing. This would be the last time Jesus, the Son of God, visited the temple. The temple was eventually destroyed in 70 AD.

Verses 3-37. After leaving the temple, four of the disciples gather around Jesus for a private audience. They ask Jesus to tell about the destruction of the temple and what signs might they expect when this was about to happen. For the disciples and many others, the destruction of the temple was paramount to the end of time and the coming of the full reign of God. Both Matthew and Luke record this prophetic teaching but with varying details.

Instead of confirming that the destruction of the temple would usher in the reign of God, Jesus gave the disciples a warning (*vs. 5*). Jesus cautions that many will come claiming to be from the Son of God and thus lead many astray. The Lord goes on to say that there will be wars with nations rising up against nation but the end is not yet here. These are only "birth-pangs" (*vs. 8*). This would be a reference to a woman having contractions just prior to going into labor. The symbolism would normally be announcing the closeness or nearness of the new age. But as it is used here, it seems to be more like what we call "false labor." Certainly, the time is near, but not just yet. There is more pain and greater agony to come.

In the midst of outlining the various trials and tribulations that were to come, Jesus affirms that the Gospel must first be preached to all nations (*vs. 10*). As is typical of the entire message of the Old and New Testament, judgment does not come before an opportunity to repent is offered. The Good News of Jesus will be proclaimed to all prior to the final judgment and glorious Return of Christ. While many will be persecuted for proclaiming the Gospel, they will not need to worry about what to say before their accusers, as the Holy Spirit will direct their words.

Jesus continues His prophetic pronouncement by citing something similar to Daniel's apocalyptic vision (Daniel 9:27; 11:31; 12:11). It is not clear if Jesus is referring to another future sacrilege, perhaps by the Romans, but Daniel's vision did come true when Antiochus Epiphanes brought pagan idols into the temple and forced unclean sacrifices. This sacrilege is credited as the cause of the Maccabees Rebellion (166 BC), which led to the reestablishment of Israel as a nation. This is a very simplistic version of historical events, but was obviously a high note in Jewish history.

Jesus then makes an astounding statement. If the Lord had not shortened the days of tribulation no humans would have survived (*vs. 20*)! For the sake of the elect the Lord stopped the horrible events that were happening. That word "elect" has caused a great deal of trouble for the church down through history. Please note two things in Jesus' apocalyptic vision. The elect, do not avoid the trials and evils Jesus foresaw. Neither were the elect the only ones saved by the Lord's intervention. Jesus immediately warns that false prophets will come with signs and wonders with further attempts to lead the elect away.

After the tribulation has ended, Jesus seems to predict a cataclysmic cosmic event. Whether we are to take these words literally or figuratively are not clear, but frightening nonetheless. It is then that the Son of Man will come in the clouds with great power and glory.

The term, "the Son of Man" (*vs. 26*) is used in both the Old and New Testament. It has varying uses and meaning. The term alone could be the source of an entire book and thus cannot be covered fully here. In Daniel the Son of Man is an apocalyptic figure that comes to restore Israel, but not exclusively a messiah figure. In the four Gospels the phrase is only used by Jesus, with one exception where the crowd ask Him what He means by it. Comparing the phrase "the Son of Man" with "the Son of God" would be a worthwhile study. Jesus' use of the phrase here is clearly referring to a messianic figure, who will have the angels call together all His followers, both alive and dead.

Jesus closes out His pronouncement by pleading with the disciples to remain watchful and vigilant. Here we find one of the most controversial statements recorded in the Bible. Jesus says, "…this generation will not pass away before all these things take place" (*vs. 30*). The Greek word for generation is *genea*. Our modern understanding of the English word generation doesn't fit the context well here in verse 30. Today we would interpret this to mean the group of people alive at the moment. If this were the case all the things outline in the tribulation would have happened within a span of 30 to 60 years. The temple was destroyed within that time frame, but the remaining prophecy has not been fulfilled. The word can have a much broader meaning, even that of an entire era or age. It is very possible, if read in closest context, that Jesus meant that from the time the cataclysmic comic events begin through the coming of the Son of Man would be all one generation.

What is important to understand is that we cannot know the day or hour when it will happen, thus speculation on what the word "generation" means is meaningless. Only the Father (God) knows when it will all come to fulfillment. Ours is to take heed, watch and pray. The only part of this whole prophecy that we have any control over is to proclaim the Gospel to the entire world!

Jesus At Odds:

1. Jesus predicted that the Jewish temple would be destroyed. What do you think the disciples' first reaction was?

2. Once Jesus made the pronouncement about the temple two of the disciples asked two questions. What do you read behind those questions?

3. How do you think the disciples felt when they learned that neither the angels nor Jesus knew when the end would come?

You At Odds:

1. Jesus said the gospel must be preached to all the nations before the end will come. What should you be doing in preparation for the return of Christ?

2. Do you believe the end is near and this generation will see Christ's return?

3. Are you watching for Christ's return? What are you doing to be alert and on guard?

NOTES

LESSON 14:

THE BETRAYAL

READ: CHAPTER 14:1-72

Prayer: *Most Powerful God, our Heavenly Father – how often have we betrayed You and Your Son? How many times, with our words and our actions have we denied our faith in and love for Jesus? As we read and study the difficult words of Jesus' betrayal, give us ears to hear and eyes to see the truth. Again, we call on Your Holy Spirit to fill us with a special gift to understand what happened to Jesus then and is still happening today. Father, give us strength and courage to remain steadfast in our faith and our loyalty to Your Son and our Savior. In Jesus' powerful name, receive our prayer. AMEN*

Mark's retelling of the betrayal of Jesus may seem rather lengthy, but in typical Mark fashion it is the shortest of the Gospel accounts. There are many details but not a word is wasted. As we've learned before, the chapter and verse markings are not original with Mark. As we move through this section you will find that my divisions may not coincide with the markings within your translation.

Verses 1-2. Mark uncharacteristically is precise with the dating of this section, two days before the Passover. We know already that there was a plot to kill Jesus since the day He rode into Jerusalem on Palm Sunday. The religious leaders apparently had no fear of God in planning to kill Jesus, but they did fear the crowds. They decided not to kill Jesus during the feast, but their plans were changed by Judas' offer of betrayal, but more so as fulfillment of prophesy.

The Passover and the Feast of Unleavened Bread normally followed one right after the other, but the celebration would last for seven days. Passover was as much a nationalistic and patriotic event as it was religious. It marked the time when God freed His people from foreign captivity, which began the journey into the Promised Land. The Romans would be on high alert for any uprising. We also know from history there was already a group of zealots, of whom Judas was a part, already planning to attempt an overthrow of the Romans occupying their land. One of the groups called themselves *am ha-aretz* or Jews of the Land. They were not particularly religious, but their sense of nationality was tied up in having the land that God had given them. They were awaiting the coming of a political messiah and Passover was the expected time of this Messiah's revealing. While Jesus taught otherwise, many believed He was this political liberator.

Verses 3-9. Jesus has arrived at the home of Simon the leper. John's Gospel goes on to identify this as the home of Lazarus, Martha and Mary. There are many things left unsaid in this verse. Is Simon still alive or confined in a leper colony? Or is Simon one of the lepers that were healed by Jesus? We do know that Lazarus was raised from the dead and again, according to John's account, this was a deciding point for the plot to kill Jesus (and Lazarus). What we do know is that Jesus was very close to this family. The similarities of the events found in Luke 7:36-50 are many, adding another layer of uncertainty to the specifics of the characters involved.

It was a Jewish custom to wash a guest's feet and to anoint the head with a bit of oil, but the woman in Mark's account certainly exceeded the normal courtesy. The details that Mark offers are important. The oil was enclosed in an alabaster flask signifying that is was probably a family heirloom passed down from mother to daughter. The oil was pure nard (or spikenard), which was imported from India further indicating its value. We would not, however, know the real value had Judas not declared it for us.

This was a wealthy family that welcomed Jesus and His disciples into their home. The oil used to anoint Jesus was valued at an average year's salary! It certainly would have gone a long way in supporting Jesus' ministry or Judas' revolt. Mark does not identify Judas as the one who indignantly scolded the woman, but John's gospel does. Noteworthy, you do not find Martha or Lazarus complaining about Mary's extravagance. It was an act of adoration as much as a declaration of love for the Lord. Like the poor woman who gave two mites to the temple treasury Jesus identifies this gift as worthy of praise.

While the argument that the oil could have been sold to give support to the poor may have been insincere, it led Jesus to state that they would always have the poor among them, but they would not always have Him. Jesus often gave preference to the poor so at first glance this statement seems a little surprising. But He makes a critical point. Our personal acts of piety can never take the place of genuine adoration for our Lord. Altruistic deeds are simply the acts of do-gooders if they are not grounded in genuine faith and love for the Lord.

Jesus made another clear reference to His impending death and even offered a foreshadowing of the fact that the normal funeral rituals would not be accomplished. Jesus declared the anointing as preparation for His burial.

Verses 10-11. Without fanfare or detailed explanation, Mark has Judas exiting the house and going to the chief priest. It almost seems as Judas made his decision to betray Jesus either as the result of being reprimanded about the poor or due to the waste of the value the nard. The fact that Judas provided the Jewish leadership an opportunity to carry out their plot, their plan to wait until after the feast was altered and God's plan continued on track.

Verses 12-50. Judas' betrayal of Jesus is outlined in four sections beginning with the preparations for the Last Supper and ending with Jesus being seized by temple guards. Again, as is Mark's style, he segments a simple recording of the facts with little or no hidden symbolism.

Two unnamed disciples are sent by Jesus into town to make preparations for the Passover meal. The ritualistic meal would begin at sunset. By established rules, there would need to be at least 10 persons present for the Passover meal. The disciples were instructed to meet with a man carrying a jar of water and then follow him to the location for the meal. Much has been made of a man carrying a water jar, as this was normally considered women's work. The suggestion is such a person would be easy to spot.

The location of the upper room seems to be a place other than Mary and Martha's home in which they were being hosted. It must, however, have been close to the Mount of Olives and the Garden of Gethsemane. While history and tradition suggest certain locations, it is impossible to pinpoint with absolute assurance. Mark also seems to infer that the man carrying the water and the homeowner are not the same person. History places the Upper Room or Cenacle on Mt. Zion, which is across the Kidron Valley.

Verse 17-21. It is during the Passover meal that Jesus announces that one of the twelve is a traitor. Mark offers none of the pre-meal details that other Gospel writers do. Neither does Mark give us details of who the betrayer is other than one dipping bread into the dish with him (see verse 10 above). It almost seems that Mark presumes the readers know the story.

Verses 22-25. During the meal Jesus varies the traditional Passover liturgy and creates for us a new covenant. Jesus adding these words to the ritual would certainly have been a shock to the disciples. Interestingly, the words Jesus adds are very reminiscent of the Jewish wedding vows given by both the groom and bride. This new sacrament is declaring that Jesus is the sacrificial lamb taking away the sins of the world. It also has a strong hint that Jesus was declaring Himself the Bridegroom and His followers, both present and future, will be the glorious bride. His reference to drinking the fruit of the vine in the new Kingdom of God recalls the consistent image of the great wedding feast that will usher in the new era.

Verses 26-52. After the meal was over and hymns were sung, the group left the upper room and crossed over the valley to the Garden of Gethsemane. Again, it would be hard to pinpoint the location of the garden, but tradition has it being at the foot of the

Mount of Olives. The Garden of Gethsemane marks the final two movements in the betrayal of Jesus.

Jesus foretold the disciples that they would all scatter once He was arrested, thus fulfilling prophecy (Zechariah 13:7). Jesus again, states that He will be raised up, but the disciples seem not to hear it. Peter immediately boasts that he will not abandon Jesus, but is met with the dire prediction that he, Peter, will deny Jesus three times before the sun is up. Peter protests his loyalty, as do the remaining 10 disciples.

Mark's account of the Garden of Gethsemane events is rather short. It does, however, list two significant features. The first is that Jesus was personally troubled by the coming crucifixion. He prayed to God using the childlike endearment "Abba." Jesus was pleading with His Daddy to spare His life if it were at all possible. But remarkably, in the midst of that heart-wrenching plea, Jesus would not accept any solution for Himself that was not the will of His Father. Obedience, even in the face of death.

Embedded within this moving prayer scene is the fact that the disciples could not remain awake. Jesus took three of the disciples aside with Him to pray. His instructions were to remain and watch (stay awake). Twice Jesus found them sleeping.

There has been much speculation and many sermons on this passage. Why are these facts recorded? The simplest answer would be that this is just a continuation of the prediction that the disciples could not remain with Jesus and that they all would fall away. Here, they couldn't even stay awake. Another suggestion has been made that in keeping with the Passover story, the people were to stay ready to depart Egypt immediately after the Death Angel "passed over" them. The disciples were unable to maintain the symbolic readiness of the memorial feast.

In the disciples' defense, they had just completed a very large meal where the ritual required that none of the food be left over. It was also very late into the night. Jesus knew full well what was about to happen, but the disciples still did not understand the immediacy of the moment. After finding them asleep the second time, Jesus declared that the time had come and the betrayer had arrived.

As prearranged by Judas (and prophecy) he came with a "crowd" of the religious elite. Included among them were the Chief Priests, scribes, and elders. Also among them were what appear to be members of the temple guard carrying weapons. With the agreed upon sign Judas kissed Jesus and the guards seized Jesus. There was a token resistance and symbolically an ear was cut off. Jesus quelled the skirmish so that prophecy might be fulfilled and God's will be accomplished. In typical Mark brevity, "And they all forsook Him and fled."

Verses 51-52. These verses are unique to Mark with no apparent ties to other gospel stories about Jesus. There have been many speculative suggestions, some even bizarre, but there is no specific confirmation of who this young man is. Probably the simplest to accept is that the man was John Mark himself. If the Upper Room was the home of Mary, John Mark's mother (a location where the disciple were known to have met: Acts 12:12) it might be that the author arose from his sleep and followed the disciples to Gethsemane, offering this embarrassing story as authentication of an eye witness account to Jesus' arrest.

Verses 53-72. The crowd that seized Jesus in the garden led Him to the High Priest. Peter had followed the entourage right into the High Priest's courtyard. The full council of priests and elders had come together to receive testimony against Jesus. Their plans to wait until after the festival was over to seize Jesus had been altered by Judas' offer of betrayal. Please remember, however, that it is still in the wee hours of the morning while it was still quite dark that the council came together to interrogate Jesus. This was still a very secret meeting that was taking place.

Jewish law required at least two witness to agree before any crime could be attested to a person (Numbers 35:30, Deuteronomy 19:15). Mark repeatedly states that the various witnesses could not agree. Interestingly, the testimony of a false witness was punishable by the same fate sought after for the innocent person. By their own laws the religious elite were all subject to be crucified. Finally, the High Priest asked Jesus if He was the Christ and Jesus answered plainly "I am."

John's gospel account outlines a strong and clear theme based on Jesus' use of the phrase "I am." This is the name God gave for Himself to Moses at the burning bush scene (Exodus 3:1-15).

Mark does not offer such a strong theme, but does have Jesus using the "I am" phrase here. The New Testament usage of *ego eimi* (I am) is a self-confession by Jesus that He is the Son of God, the Christ, and the Messiah. At Jesus' personal declaration of Who He truly is, the High Priest cries "blasphemy."

The scene then shifts to Peter in the courtyard. Peter was confronted by those standing by as being one of Jesus' disciples. Three times he was confronted and three times Peter denied knowing Jesus. As foretold by Jesus, upon the third denial the cock crowed. The final phrase in the NRSV is "And he broke down and wept." The meaning of the Greek is a bit unclear. Several commentators have opted to accept a meaning that Peter covered his face and wept. This was apparently a common expression of sadness and remorse, pulling one's coat over the head and weeping. Regardless of the exact meaning, the last we see of Peter in Mark's gospel is him rushing out of the courtyard of the high priest totally broken by his failure and denial.

Jesus At Odds:

1. What was Jesus at odds with when the woman was anointing His head with the expensive perfume? Did Jesus experience any conflict over this beautiful act?

2. Knowing full well who was to betray Him, how did Jesus continue with the Lord's Supper?

3. Why did Jesus stay in Gethsemane so long? Why didn't He run and hide?

4. What or who was Peter at odds with while following Jesus into the courtyard?

You At Odds:

1. Have you ever sold out Jesus like Judas? Have you ever denied Jesus like Peter?

2. Would you have stayed once they arrested Jesus? Have you ever fled before?

3. While not fully cited in Mark, what was the ultimate difference between Judas and Peter's response to their failure? What has been your response?

NOTES

LESSON 15:

THE FINAL CONFLICT

READ: CHAPTER 15:1 – 16:8

Prayer: *Our Heavenly Father – We arrive to this point with heavy hearts, feeling the full weight of Peter's shame and guilt. We, ourselves, have been in Peter sandals so many times and in so many situations! But we praise You that we are not left in the darkness of the High Priest's courtyard. Take us now to the cross. Let us see the horror, but let us also see, feel, and accept for ourselves the love and power that Jesus' cross now represents. Lead us from the cross to the grave. Let us celebrate the victory of the empty tomb. Let us recapture our voices and sing Your praises! Hear our prayer. AMEN.*

Generally, the Roman government let the local religious authorities dish out punishment upon those guilty of violating some religious law. However, the death penalty was reserved solely for Roman authority. The religious leaders wanted Jesus dead, but lest they test the resolve of the Roman occupiers they could not kill Jesus. Once the council reached an agreement they delivered Jesus to Pilate, the local Roman governor.

Pilate interrogated Jesus at length citing the many different charges the religious leaders had placed upon Him. Mark's account of Jesus before Pilate is very short and limited, but still gives us the feel that Pilate really didn't want to have to deal with Jesus.

All four gospels suggest that there was a custom for the Roman Governor to release someone condemned to death during the Passover celebration. This was called the Paschal Pardon. Interestingly, there is no non-Biblical historical account of this ever happening.

Pilate asks the crowd if they would like him to release Jesus or someone in His place. The crowd, stirred up by the religious leaders, call for Barabbas to be released. According to Mark Barabbas was charged with murder during an insurrection or riot. It seems highly unlikely that Pilate would consider releasing someone involved in an insurrection against the Roman forces as this would subject him to punishment by Caesar. There does seem to be something else involved in this scene, however.

The full name of the person offered for release was "Yeshua Bar Abba." This reads in certain manuscripts of Matthew's gospel as Jesus Barabbas or Jesus, son of the father! Was Pilate trying to play a joke on the people? Is this some kind of "parable" that the authors of all four Gospels are offering? Or is this perhaps a symbolic comparison between the political and spiritual Messiah? Add to this a cynical note. Jesus was a common name in those days. Barabbas, however, was a common name for someone who didn't know who his or her father was.

Regardless of what can or cannot be made of the name Barabbas, it is clear that the Jewish leadership wanted Jesus (of Nazareth) killed. They shouted for Him to be crucified. The implication that the religious leaders were advocating crucifixion is even more telling in that according to Jewish law a religious curse was inherent in this form of execution (Deuteronomy 21:23).

Verses 16-47. Once Pilate turned Jesus over to the Roman soldiers, they mocked Him. They placed a purple robe on Jesus and crown of thorns on His head continuing their mockery. Purple came from an expensive dye that came only from the island of Pompeii and thus the color was a sign of royalty or wealth. When the soldiers tired of their derision and ridicule, they led Jesus out to be crucified.

The Roman soldiers commanded Simon of Cyrene to carry Jesus' cross. Under Roman law a soldier was permitted to commandeer someone to carry a load up to one mile (see Matthew 5:41).

In all probability Simon and his sons, Alexander and Rufus, were known by the early Christians who would be reading Mark's gospel account. There is a Rufus mentioned in Romans 16:13 and there is a Simon (Simeon) of Niger mentioned in Acts 13. We know from history that there was a large Jewish and later Christian community in Cyrene located on the Northern shore of Africa (Libya). We also know that the Cyrenians started the church in Antioch. While this is little more than conjecture, there seems to be a close connection between these Biblical characters. While the scriptures are truly colorblind, and Mark certainly makes no distinction, it highly possible that the Simon of Cyrene who carried Jesus' cross was a Black man.

All four Gospels record Jesus being brought to the hill called Golgotha. If you look up pictures of the site you can see where the locals might call it the place of the skull. The KJV of the Bible uses the Latin name Calvary. Mt. Calvary sounds so much better in songs and poems than either Golgotha or the skull. The hill was located just outside the gates of Jerusalem.

They offered Jesus wine mingled with myrrh. Jesus denied the drink as He had already pledged not to drink it again until the establishment of the new Kingdom. There does appear to be a custom of giving this mixture as an opiate or sedative to lessen the horror of the crucifixion. It was also the custom to give wine to those in distress. Psalm 31:6ff tells of an interesting custom of giving strong drink to the poor to help them forget their poverty. Mark continues with a very brief account of the soldiers gambling for His clothes. Mark indicates that they crucified Jesus at the third hour (three hours after sun up which would have been about 9:00am). This was the time of morning when the priest should have been taking the daily sacrifices and the time when the Sanhedrin would be seated for their daily judgments. Instead they were as the foot of the cross casting insults and mocking Jesus.

Mark also briefly records the fact that Jesus was hung between two criminals. Some ancient transcripts insert a verse that reads *And the scripture was fulfilled which says, "He was reckoned with the transgressors.* This would have been more in keeping with Matthew's style as he consistently showed how the events of Jesus life were fulfillment of scripture. There was an inscription placed over the head of the criminals citing their crime for which they were receiving the death penalty. In Jesus' case is simply said "The King of the Jews."

At the sixth hour (noon) there was a darkness that covered the whole land. The word could be appropriately translated *the whole earth.* It would be impossible to determine what kind of cosmic event this was, as it lasted for three hours. Many have claimed an eclipse, which may be possible because it was the time of a full moon. A full eclipse, however, lasts only a very short time due to the rotation of the earth. The earth would have had to stop its rotation for a period of three hours, which would have cause numerous other events to have occurred. It should be noted that many historical achieves record the period of darkness.

At the ninth hour (3:00pm) Jesus cried out and many thought He was calling for Elijah. They gave Jesus a vinegar-filled sponge to drink. This was to keep Him awake much in the same manner as breaking an ammonia capsule under someone's nose to revive him or her to his or her senses. They wanted to see if Elijah would return. At the moment of Jesus' death He cried out again and *breathed His last.* Mark does not recount the earth shaking or tombs being opened, but he does record that the veil in the temple was torn in two.

The symbolism of the torn veil is that through the sacrifice that Jesus offered through His death on the cross, we now have unhindered access to God the Heavenly Father. Equally so for the Jewish people, the traditions that separated the religious elite from the rest of God's people had been destroyed. The truth of their ungodliness had been unveiled and they were no longer "set apart" from the people.

The ninth hour was also the time that the daily sacrifice offered earlier would be slain. Jesus, because of His death on the cross, became the ultimate sacrifice. There was no longer any need for multiple lambs to be slain because Christ was offered "once for all" (Hebrews 10:1-10, 1 Peter 3:18).

This section concludes with a declaration by the Centurion that Jesus was the "Son of God."

While Jesus' own people didn't recognize Him, the Roman gentile did. We find in Acts and other places in the New Testament favorable mention of a Centurion, perhaps the same one who was at the foot of the Cross.

Verses 40-47. Many have tried to consolidate the information found in the four gospels to determine who the women at the cross were. Luke gives no names, while Matthew, Mark and John do. Mary Magdalene is mentioned in all three accounts. Mary the mother of James and Joses is mentioned in Matthew and Mark. John specifically mentions Jesus' mother and Mary, the wife of Clopas. Salome is mentioned by Mark whose name he may have used to try to distinguish between the various Marys.

Late on Friday evening Joseph of Arimathea approached Pilot requesting the body of Jesus. Being the day before the Sabbath they wished to take Jesus down from the cross and put Him in a tomb. Two things are at play here. The Jewish tradition was to have the body buried within 24 hours of death. While the Romans often left crucified persons on the cross for more than a day, the Jews would have frown on the bodies being left over the Sabbath and during the Passover/festival week. Pilate, accepting his centurion's report that Jesus was dead, gave permission for Joseph to take the body. Tradition has it that Nicodemus helped Joseph and they placed Jesus in a tomb owned by Joseph.

There are many legends concerning the person of Joseph of Arimathea, many of which cannot be confirmed. Mark describes him as a member of the council, presumably meaning the Sanhedrin. If this was the case, Joseph was probably rich, which also provided access to Pilate. We know from other gospel accounts that Nicodemus was a Pharisee, but at a minimum respected Jesus and His teachings.

Verses 16:1 – 8. In eight short verses, Mark gives his brief account of the Resurrection. The same three women Mark had at the foot of the cross are now reintroduced. The Sabbath was officially over at sundown on Saturday. The women waited until early Sunday when it began to be light to return to the tomb with spices. Mark records that Joseph had wrapped Jesus in a linen cloth, but does not mention the spices that Nicodemus brought. The women were coming to finish the duties of preparing Jesus' body.

The women, knowing where Jesus was laid, wondered among themselves who would move the stone covering the tomb. When arriving at the tomb they discovered that the stone was already moved. They encountered a young man whose description and clothing indicated that he was a heavenly messenger or angel.

The angel gave them the message that Jesus was alive. He was risen. The angel instructed the women to go tell the disciples that Jesus would see them again in Galilee. One notable difference was the angel told them to tell the disciples *and Peter*. At first glance it would seem that Peter was no longer considered one of the disciples because of his denials. The statement serves as a clear pronouncement that Peter was to personally receive the news that Jesus was risen from the dead, perhaps a proclamation of Peter being forgiven. If Mark's gospel is as many believe, a recap of Peter's preaching, this certainly would have been a significant part of Peter's message.

The angel's instructions include a clear expectation of post-resurrection appearances by Jesus. The angel clearly states that Jesus is going on ahead to Galilee where the disciples *will see Him*. The majority of commentators believe that verse eight (8) concludes Mark's writings. It seem rather abrupt and ends with the women fleeing in fear and telling no one, contrary to the angel's instructions. The word "afraid" can be softened by taking the meaning as an emotional state brought on by a sense of worship and awe, or in this case amazement or astonishment. As for the silence of the women, most commentators indicate that they told no one on their way to where the disciples were hiding (Matthew 28.8, Luke 24:9-11, 22-24).

Second Ending of Mark (16:9-20) No one knows exactly how the remaining verses of Mark's gospel account got added or when, but most agree that they could not have been part of the regular text. Ending at verse 8 does seem to be abrupt, but not totally uncharacteristic of Mark's style. In recording the basic narrative from which Peter preached, the Resurrection was a given and not something needing to be proven. While we know from the other gospel writers, the women did go tell the disciples, but Mark's ending is in total agreement with *The Gospel of Peter*, which was not canonized by the church fathers.

One early authority adds the following after verse 8: *But they reported briefly to Peter and those with him all that they had been told. And after this, Jesus Himself sent out by means of them, from east to west, the sacred and imperishable proclamation of eternal salvation.* While nothing here disagrees with the overall gospel story, scholars generally conclude that these were not the words of Mark.

If there were additional verses outline post-resurrection appearance by Jesus attached to Mark's gospel, they were lost very soon after the Gospel was written. Under what conditions or circumstance they were lost is beyond historical account. Many manuscripts, some very ancient, end the gospel with verses 9-20 showing that they were accepted by the early church and consequently canonized by church leaders.

Verses 9-18. Mary Magdalene is clearly associated with the women who were at the cross and later came to the tomb. Jesus casting out *Seven Demons* is confirmed by the other gospel writers. Jesus appeared to Mary Magdalene first and then Mark records what appears to be a reference to Jesus' appearance on the road to Emmaus (Luke 24:13-35). The Emmaus road appearance was to Cleopas and a companion. While unidentified either in Mark or Luke, this companion could easily have been Cleopas' wife who is identified as one of the women who returned to the tomb.

Jesus then appears to the eleven where He "upbraided" them for their doubt, very reminiscent of John's characterization of Jesus' post-resurrection appearance. Jesus then gives the disciples the commission to preach the gospel to all of creation. The accompaniment of "signs" such as casting out demons (Acts 8:6-7), speaking in tongues (Acts 2:37-42, 1 Corinthians 14:2-5) and healing (Acts 28:8, James 5:13-16) are all attested to in the early church. Picking up snakes and drinking poison without harm to believers has no specific New Testament parallel. There is a reference of Paul being bit by a viper in Acts 28:3-6 but not by intentionally testing his faith. Drinking poison has a few second century references in Christian literature, but none in the New Testament.

Jesus' exaltation into heaven seated at the right hand of God has many New Testament counterparts and thus can be attested to by the earliest hymns of the Church. For Mark, this was understood. Jesus died. Jesus rose from the grave. Jesus is alive forever more. For Mark this was not the end of the Good News – this was only the beginning!

Jesus At Odds:

1. Why did Jesus continue to go through the interrogation by Pilate and the torture that followed when He could have commanded the angles to rescue Him?

2. Who or what was Pilate at odds with during the trial of Jesus?

3. Who or what was God the Father at odds with during the hours of darkness? Who won the conflict?

You At Odds:

1. If you were Mary (any of the Mary's) could you have remained at the foot of the cross?

2. Who do you best represent: Joseph of Arimathea – the Centurion – Mary Magdalene?

3. Are you still looking for Jesus who was crucified or are you worshiping the Risen Christ, look for His glorious return?

NOTES

EPILOGUE: STILL AT ODDS?

Mark was clearly writing to an audience who was at odds with the world around them. They were believers of the Risen Christ. Little did Mark realize that some 2000 years later the believers of the Risen Christ would still be at odds with the world. Some of today's readers are like Jesus and His disciples, still at odds with the religious elite. But I feel the strong words of encouragement that Mark intended. We do worship the Risen Christ. While there may still be conflict the war is over and the battle won!

Christ has died – Christ is Risen – Christ will come again!

Closing Prayer: *Most gracious and Loving God – You are so awesome, so powerful, yet so loving. You gave up Your only Son to face the evil and hatred of this world, even to the point of death on a cross. You gave Him up for us, though He died that we might live. Oh, how You must love us! As we walked with Jesus through the eyes of Mark we experienced His struggles, we faced His disappointments, only to realize we were the source of all that pain. We are humbled at the extravagant price You paid for us. We can never repay You so we simply give You our hearts and lives. What Jesus was as He walked this earth – let us be for You now. Not the Son of God, but sons and daughters of a loving Father. Empower us with Your Holy Spirit that we might go into all the world and preach the Good News to all creation. Hear our prayers and receive them in the Name above all names – Jesus Christ. AMEN!*

Appendix A:

Participatory Study Method

How can I get more from my Bible reading?

There is no shortcut in Bible study. If you want to find what God has for you in Scripture you will have to dig. There are some things you can do to make your study time more profitable. In this appendix you will find an outline to an approach to Bible study that can help you both with devotional reading and with deeper study.

PREPARATION

Gather Materials – have pen, paper, highlighters or other markers and all materials you will need for study available.

Conditions – Find a place where you can study. If you study well with music playing, put some on. If you prefer quiet, arrange for a quiet place.

Resources – Get a small, well-selected set of study materials. For suggestions see the resource list in Appendix B.

Prayer – As you begin your study, consider the premise that Scripture comes to us as God-breathed, and therefore it is "useful for teaching for reproof, for correction, and for training in righteousness, so that everyone who belongs to God may be proficient, equipped for every good work" (2 Timothy 3:16- 17 NRSV). Keeping in mind this word, share in this prayer:

> *Eternal God, in the reading of the Scripture, may your word be heard; in the meditations of our hearts, may your*

word be known; and in the faithfulness of our lives, may your word be shown. Amen.

(Chalice Worship, 384).

GET AN OVERVIEW OF THE PASSAGE

Read the passage multiple times. Any number from three times up will help. Memorizing is useful, at least of key texts. (This will also require you to select key texts.) Read from different Bible versions, to help you with your concentration, and to open up different ways of understanding the passage. At this point don't use commentaries, study notes, your concordance, or anything which takes your concentration off of the passage you are studying.

STUDY THE BACKGROUND

Find out who wrote the passage, to whom it was written, what is the situation being addressed, and what type of literature it is.

MEDITATE, QUESTION, RESEARCH, COMPARE (REPEAT AS NEEDED)

Meditate on the passage. If you are having difficulty meditating, think about telling someone else about the passage, such as a friend in need of encouragement, someone who is struggling with their faith or asking questions about faith, or a child. Think: What questions might they ask about this passage? You can formulate thought questions or fact questions. Fact questions focus on what the author is actually saying. Thought questions may lead you to other revelations that lay well beyond the intended statement of the passage.

You might consider creating an outline of the passage, compare it with other Scriptures or with the writings of figures in church history, or even to current experience.

Ask: What similar experience are we having today? Could this help me better understand the passage. For example, if you have had a vision, might this help you understand the vision recorded in Ezekiel 1? Ask your friends about experiences they have had. You might consult historical figures such as: Jerome, Aquinas, Teresa of Avila, Augustine, Martin Luther, John Wesley, John Calvin, Karl Barth, and many others.

SHARE YOUR THOUGHTS

Ask yourself how this text has been applied in your experience. Get to know the person you are sharing with. Share your experience and then the text. Always work from your own personal experience with God. Store up the experiences your friends share with you to use in studying further Scripture.

The purpose of sharing is not just to help others with your own insight. It is also intended to provide a check on what you think you have learned. It is easy to get off track in independent Bible study. Sharing helps keep you a part of the community. Make sure that some of your sharing is with people who have experience and training in study. Training and degrees do not guarantee accuracy, but it does provide a valuable check.

EXAMPLE PASSAGE 1 KINGS 19:11-18

1. Begin your study with prayer.
2. Read the passage several times. Can you tell this story in your own words?
   a) Read 1 Kings 17-19. Check a Bible dictionary or study Bible for the background of 1Kings.
   b) Consider how Elijah feels through this experience.
   c) Consider what God is trying to accomplish by giving Elijah these experiences.
   d) How did Elijah know the Lord was not in the wind, the earthquake or the fire?
   e) Can the Lord appear in such violent events? (Use your concordance, looking up wind, fire, and earthquake.)
   f) Does God respond to Elijah's complaint? (Only indirectly; he gives him a task.)

g)   Is Elijah as much alone as he feels he is? (No, there are 7,000 more faithful people, v. 18.)

h)   What other Bible characters have experienced something similar to this? (Daniel 3—the fiery furnace.)

i)   What people in church history may have experienced something similar to this? (Any martyr or person who has suffered persecution.)

j)   Have you experienced similar feelings? Have you ever felt completely alone in your faith?

3.   Share your experiences!!

EXAMPLE PRAYER FOR BIBLE STUDY

Lord, take from me any thought habits which will keep me from hearing. Make me open to your voice and your voice alone. Lord, help me to accept your people as my brothers and sisters in your kingdom and let me learn and grow from both their weaknesses and their strengths. Lord, I trust you to reveal yourself to your people the way you know is best. Let your will be done. Lord, let me not only recognize but obey your voice. Let my actions be conformed to your will. Help me to love my neighbor as myself. In Jesus' name, Amen.

APPENDIX B:

TOOLS FOR BIBLE STUDY

The following are some suggested resources for Bible study. They fall into eight categories:

BIBLE VERSIONS

You will need a Bible version that you can understand without having to consult an English dictionary too often.

✓ For quick reading (overview):

» *Contemporary English Version* (CEV)

3rd or 4th grade reading level; high degree of accuracy within the context of its aim for easy readability.

» *The Cotton Patch Version* by Clarence Jordan

An interpretive paraphrase reflecting rural Georgian dialect and culture.

» *The Message*

Heavily paraphrased with cultural terms translated. This version is fun to read, but will tend to obscure elements of the original cultures.

» *New Living Translation* (NLT)

A more accurate revision of the Living Bible. This is the easy-reading Bible for evangelical Christians.

» *Today's New International Version*

Shows its relationship to the popular NIV in many wordings, but uses simplified language and sentence structure in many cases.

✓ For study or reading:

» *Common English Bible* (CEB)

A new translation sponsored by Mainline Protestant publishing houses, the CEB attempts to combine high level scholarship with readability. The New Testament was published in 2010, with the complete Bible available in 2011.

» *New International Version* (NIV)

The NIV is a dynamic equivalent translation of the Bible that is popular among evangelical Christians. A new revision of this translation appeared in electronic form in 2010 and will be available in print in 2011

» *New Revised Standard Version* (NRSV)

The descendant of the Revised Standard Version, it is the Bible of choice for mainline Christians needing a study Bible. It is known for its attempt to use gender neutral language where appropriate.

» *Revised English Bible* (REB)

This version was translated by an interdenominational committee with interfaith review, that exhibits the different texture of British English.

» *New American Standard Bible* (NASB)

A very formal rendering of the original languages, the NASB has its roots in conservative evangelicalism. It can be wooden and difficult to read.

STUDY BIBLES

Study Bibles usually contain introductory articles giving Bible backgrounds, information on methodology and overviews of various themes in the Bible. They will also include introductions to each book and comments on difficult passages. Study Bibles will reflect religious views of editors and authors, some more than others. Care should be taken to distinguish the Biblical text from the comments, and facts and opinions within the comments.

✓   *New Interpreter} Study Bible* (NRSV)

This new study Bible includes extensive historical and theological annotations, good introductions and outlines, and excursuses giving further background and insight regarding particular themes and passages.

✓   *New Oxford Annotated Bible* (NRSV)

A standard scholarly study Bible, often used in universities and seminaries.

✓   *HarperCollins Study Bible* (NRSV)

Carrying the sponsorship of the Society of Biblical Literature, it has Mainstream or liberal notes with acknowledgment of more conservative options.

✓   *Oxford Study Bible* (REB)

✓   *The NIV Study Bible* (Zondervan)

Popular among evangelicals, bringing a more conservative approach to the Bible.

✓   *ESV Study Bible*

A new Reformed standard study.

✓   *NLT Study Bible*

Based on the popular, easy-to-read New Living Translation, this evangelical study Bible provides extensive notes on both background and application.

BIBLE HANDBOOKS

Bible handbooks provide historical and cultural information, usually with a number of general articles and then comments on particular books and passages. Using a Bible handbook along with your Bible is like having a Bible with study notes, though usually having a handbook in a separate volume will mean that the handbook contains more exhaustive information. Bible handbooks, like study Bibles, will reflect religious presuppositions of the editors. Use them carefully.

✓   Mainstream and/or Liberal

»   *The Cambridge Companion to the Bible O:iford Companion to the Bible*

✓ Moderate

»   *Eerdman's Handbook to the Bible*

✓ Conservative

»   *Zondervan's Handbook to the Bible*

BACKGROUND DOCUMENTS

✓ Pritchard, James. *Ancient Near Eastern Texts*

Large, expensive, hard cover but a tremendous resource for the Bible student.

✓ Pritchard, James. *The Ancient Near East, Volume 1, An Anthology of Texts and Pictures*

(Both 1958 and 1975 editions still available)

✓ Charlesworth, James H. *The Old Testament Pseudepigrapha* (2 volumes).

This work is a standard for editions of these extra-biblical works.

BIBLE COMMENTARIES

Bible commentaries are designed to provide introductions, background, and interpretation of biblical texts. They come in many forms, ranging from one-volume efforts to commentaries on individual books. Many commentaries appear in sets, but with few exceptions, when purchasing commentaries on individual books of the Bible it is better to buy these individually rather than in sets. There are a few exceptions, such as with the New Interpreter's Bible, which is something of a hybrid. It is important to stay away from older, dated commentaries, except perhaps for devotional or theological reasons. In many online programs you will find commentaries such as Matthew Henry's, which is in public domain and thus free to publish without copyright infringement. It is, however, an 18th century product. A good place to start for any library is a solid, up-to-date one-volume commentary.

✓ Mainstream

» *New Interpreter's Bible*, 12 volumes (Abingdon)

A replacement for the venerable Interpreter's Bible, this is a mainstream commentary set drawing its authors from across the Christian community, including evangelical, mainline, Catholic, and Orthodox scholars.

» *New Interpeter's One Volume Commentary* (Abingdon)

Based on the principles of the much larger multi-volume edition, it is a completely new commentary and not simply an abridgement.

» *HarperCollins Bible Commentary* (HarperOne)

As with the HarperCollins Bible Dictionary, this commentary is sponsored by the Society of Biblical Literature.

» *People's New Testament Commentary of the New Testament* (WJK Press)

This commentary on the New Testament is written by two Disciples of Christ scholars, Fred Craddock and Eugene Boring.

» *The New Jerome Bible Commentary*, 3rd edition (Prentice Hall)

This is a predominantly Roman Catholic commentary, authored and edited by highly regarded critical scholars.

✓ Evangelical

» *Eerdmans Commentary on the Bible*

This work is very compatible with mainstream scholarship, but comes from a publisher that stands as a bridge between evangelical and mainline Protestantism.

» *New Bible Commentary: 21st Century edition* (IVP)

BIBLE CONCORDANCES

Concordances may be exhaustive, complete, or concise. Usage of these terms is not 100% consistent. In addition they may either be either organized by words or topics. Many Bibles contain small, concise concordances. Many study Bibles contain topical concordances. Exhaustive concordances contain every reference to a word listed under every word. Complete concordances contain references to each and every verse, using significant terms, though not necessarily under every word in the verse. Concise concordances contain selective references and may not reference all verses. Topical concordances provide a guide to topics covered by specific texts. This can be helpful, but one must always remember that unlike a typical concordance, which is rooted in word usage, this type is more likely to be driven by theological presuppositions.

Concordances with Greek and/or Hebrew Lexicons can be useful, but one should remember that translation is not as simple as just picking a word from a dictionary definition. Context always determines usage and meaning.

✓   Exhaustive with Greek/Hebrew
>   *Strong's Exhaustive Concordance.*

It is part of the public domain and is regularly reprinted. It is based on the KJV and an older lexicon. It's numbering system and lexicon has served as the model for other concordances

>   *The NIV Exhaustive Concordance* (Zondervan)
Based completely on the NIV, it goes beyond Strong's.

>   *New American Standard Exhaustive Concordance of the Bible/Hebrew-Aramaic and Greek Dictionaries*

>   *New American Standard Strong's Exhaustive Concordance*

Based on the Strong's Concordance system, it is keyed to the NASB.

✓   Exhaustive Concordances
>   *NRSV Concordance Unabridged* (Zondervan)
✓   Complete Concordances

>   *Cruden's Complete Concordance to the KJV.*

This is an 18th century product, but because it is public domain it is regularly reprinted.

✓   Concise Concordances

> » *The Concise Concordance to the New Revised Standard Version* (Oxford)

✓ Topical Concordances

> » *Holman Concise Topical Concordance* (Holman Reference)
> » *Topical Analysis of the Bible* (Baker)

BIBLE DICTIONARIES

Bible dictionaries provide definitions of various biblical terms, information about places and people, and introductory information about biblical books. Most information contained in a Bible handbook can be found in a Bible dictionary, but it will be organized much differently.

The religious views of authors and editors will impact the content of a Bible dictionary, as it does with a handbook or commentary. When purchasing a Bible dictionary, it is always best to purchase one that has been authored/ edited by reputable scholars, is even-handed in its approach, and is up-to-date.

✓ Mainstream

> » *HarperCollins Bible Dictionary, Revised Edition.* (HarperOne)
> » *A Dictionary of the Bible, 2nd ed.* (Oxford University Press)

Based upon the *Harper-Collins Bible Dictionary,* this is a more up-to-date expansion.

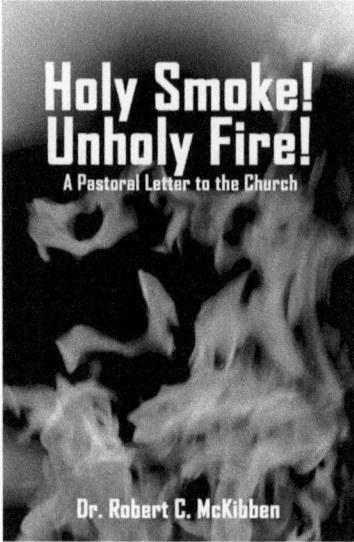

Holy Smoke! Unholy Fire! is a book so desperately needed in our time.

– Bishop William Morris
United Methodist Church

Dr. Allan Bevere has masterfully struck a perfect balance between history, theology,and modern scholarship that undergirds Paul's letters to the church in Colossi and his friend, Philemon.

– Dr. Robert C. McKibben
Retired United Methodist Pastor

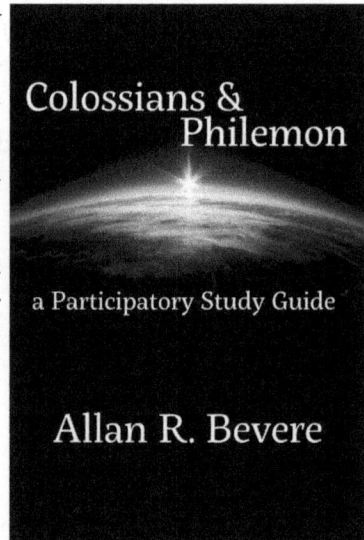

MORE FROM ENERGION PUBLICATIONS

Personal Study
Holy Smoke! Unholy Fire	Bob McKibben	$14.99
The Jesus Paradigm	David Alan Black	$17.99
When People Speak for God	Henry Neufeld	$17.99
The Sacred Journey	Chris Surber	$11.99

Christian Living
It's All Greek to Me	David Alan Black	$3.99
Grief: Finding the Candle of Light	Jody Neufeld	$8.99
My Life Story	Becky Lynn Black	$14.99
Crossing the Street	Robert LaRochelle	$16.99
Life as Pilgrimage	David Moffett-Moore	14.99

Bible Study
From Inspiration to Understanding	Edward W. H. Vick	$24.99
Philippians: A Participatory Study Guide	Bruce Epperly	$12.99
Ephesians: A Participatory Study Guide	Robert D. Cornwall	$12.99
Ecclesiastes: A Participatory Study Guide	Russell Meek	$12.99
The Jesus Manifesto	David Moffett-Moore	$9.99

Theology
Meditations on According to John	Herold Weiss	$14.99
Creation: the Christian Doctrine	Edward W. H. Vick	$12.99
Ultimate Allegiance	Robert D. Cornwall	$9.99
History and Christian Faith	Edward W. H. Vick	$9.99
The Journey to the Undiscovered Country	William Powell Tuck	$9.99
Process Theology	Bruce G. Epperly	$5.99

Ministry
Clergy Table Talk	Kent Ira Groff	$12.99
Wind and Whirlwind	David Moffett-Moore	$9.99

Generous Quantity Discounts Available
Dealer Inquiries Welcome
Energion Publications — P.O. Box 841
Gonzalez, FL 32560
Website: http://energionpubs.com
Phone: (850) 525-3916

www.ingramcontent.com/pod-product-compliance
Lightning Source LLC
LaVergne TN
LVHW041229080426
835508LV00011B/1119